Sonja Linden, the writer

Born in London to German refugee parents, Sonja is a theatre producer and writer whose plays have been produced on radio and on stage throughout the UK and the United States. She is the founding artistic director of Visible Theatre Ensemble, having previously founded iceandfire theatre (www.iceandfire.co.uk), a company that explores human rights through performance (nominated for a Liberty award in 2010). Sonja's plays for iceandfire include: *On A Clear Day You Can See Dover* (Wilton's Music Hall, Crucible Theatre, Sheffield and UK national tour), *Welcome to Ramallah*, co-written with Adah Kay, and its companion piece, *Palestine Monologues,* (Arcola Theatre, York Theatre Royal, Compass Theatre, San Diego); *Crocodile Seeking Refuge* (Lyric Hammersmith, UK national tour), *Asylum Dialogues* (Tricycle Theatre and UK national tour), *I Have Before Me a Remarkable Document Given to Me by a Young Lady from Rwanda* (Finborough Theatre, UK and USA tours, BBC World Service Radio), and *Asylum Monologues* (UK national tour). Previous work includes: *The Strange Passenger* (Paines Plough, Battersea Arts Centre and UK National Tour); *The Jewish Daughter*, sequel to Brecht's *The Jewish Wife* (New End Theatre); *Call Me Judas* (Paines Plough, Finborough Theatre) and *Present Continuous* (Edinburgh Festival, Fringe First, BBC Radio 4)

First published in the UK in 2014 by Aurora Metro Publications Ltd

67 Grove Avenue, Twickenham, TW1 4HX

www.aurorametro.com   info@aurorametro.com

Who Do We Think We Are? © 2014 Sonja Linden and Company

Cover photo image Visible actor Jasmina Daniel. Design by Sam Campbell

Production: Simon Smith

With many thanks to: Neil Gregory, Richard Turk, Suzanne Mooney, Nathan Start, Nandish Pankhania.

10 9 8 7 6 5 4 3 2 1

Printed by Berforts Information Press, Herts, UK.

ISBN: 978-1-906582-89-0

ebook version: 978-1-906582-87-6

WHO DO WE THINK WE ARE?

by

SONJA LINDEN
and
COMPANY

AURORA METRO BOOKS

Other plays by Sonja Linden
available from Aurora Metro Books:

I Have Before Me a Remarkable Document Given to Me by a Young Lady from Rwanda
ISBN 978-0-9546912-3-3
£7.99

Crocodile Seeking Refuge
ISBN 978-0-9546912-9-5
£7.99

Welcome to Ramallah, co-written with Adah Kay, in the anthology *Plays for Today by Women*
eds. Robson & Gillieron
ISBN 978-1-906582-11-1
£15.99

On Creating *"Who Do We Think We Are?"*

'To embark on a new piece is to embark on an adventure. You think you're going to discover India and you discover America.'

Ariane Mnouchkine, Founder and Artistic Director
of the Theatre du Soleil ensemble, Paris.

A key feature of Visible is that we are an ensemble, which means that we create work collaboratively, drawing on the rich experience and creativity of our performers, under the artistic leadership of writer Sonja Linden and director Sue Lefton.

Our collective endeavour to create our first piece of theatre took us on a journey through ten actors' lives across three continents and three generations. The physical starting point for that journey was a rehearsal room in 2012 in which a group of older international actors began to share their personal and family histories - a great way to bond, we thought, for a group of strangers whose only common denominator was that they were actors who were 'older'. But could it be more than a bonding exercise? Could it be the foundation for our first piece of work together?

The answer turned out to be a resounding yes. The synchronicity of finding in that one room stories that included escaping from the Warsaw Ghetto as a child, surviving the atomic bomb in Nagasaki, growing up in India under the Raj, experiencing the harsh reality of Romania under Ceauşescu, being a prisoner of war in Siberia during the Russian revolution, avoiding the draft for the Vietnam war - that is to say a host of personal stories against the backcloth of some of the major historical events of the 20th century, seemed too remarkable and rich not to take further. And so our journey of play-making, drawing on the personal and family lives and photo archives of our ensemble, was begun.

Our Thanks To:

First and foremost, to the Arts Council, whose belief in Visible as an exciting initiative and an important addition to the British theatre scene has enabled us to develop *Who Do We Think We Are?* over an 18 month period of research and development and to make this launch production possible. Our thanks also to the Gee Trust, The Backstage Trust and the Lord and Lady Lurgan Foundation.

Huge personal thanks go to Dr Paul Robinson who has been a stalwart supporter of Visible since its inception, to Mike Alfreds for his inspiring workshops, to Jude Kelly for offering us a residency at the Southbank and to Sarah J. Murray for offering us a residency at the National Theatre Studio.

A big thank you also to everyone who donated to our early crowdfunding initiative , including Sir David Hare, Howard Brenton, Laura Wade, Moris Farhi, Jonathon Chadwick, Sarah Sansom, Daniele Moyal-Sharrock, Jane Dorner, Jacqui and Keith Zerdin, Terry and Joel Cohen and many, many more.

Our thanks to Visible actor Paul Humpoletz for allowing us unique access to his father's sketches while he was a POW in Siberia, and for his father's anti-Nazi political cartoons published in Das Kleine Blatt in Austria in the 30s. Our thanks equally to all the Visible actors for the use of photographs from their family archives.

On Being Visible

'You made age beautiful and something to value and celebrate. This play is of huge value and relevance to people of all ages.'

Bruce Nixon, writer, on
Who Do We Think We Are?
National Theatre Studio, 2013.

A number of well-known older British actors including Ian McKellan, Harriet Walters and Julie Walters, to name but a few, have spoken out in recent years, deploring the dearth of opportunities for older actors. What a waste of their long years of experience and craftsmanship, and how out of synch with the increasing demographic shift in our population.

With people now living longer and leading more active lives, the need is surely even greater for older people to be represented on stage, and not just as people with mental or physical health issues, but as fully paid up members of the human race, with the desires and dreams, frustrations and joys that characterise the lives of people of all ages.

This was the dream behind the founding of Visible, a new company of older actors and theatre professionals, on a mission to create exciting, contemporary work that features older people with lives as complex and interesting as any other group of people across the age spectrum - older people who refuse to be invisible.

Biographies of the Visible Ensemble

Sue Lefton – director

Born in London, Sue originally trained as a dancer, first at The Royal Ballet School and then at the Ballet Rambert, where she was taught by Ninette De Valois and Marie Rambert respectively. She went on to train as an actress at The Central School of Speech and Drama and L'Ecole Jacques Lecoq in Paris. As a theatre director her many credits include: *A Dolls House* (Sue Lefton Productions, Time Out Drama award nomination), *Blood Wedding, The Caucasian Chalk Circle, A Winters Tale* and twelve other productions for Mercury Theatre, Colchester, *Lady from the Sea* (Bridewell Theatre), *A Mad World My Masters,* (The Globe) *Welcome to Ramallah by Sonja Linden and Adah Kay* (Arcola Theatre), and most recently a production of Peter Handke's *The Hour We Knew Nothing Of Each Other* (The Guildhall School of Music and Drama.) As well as being a theatre director, Sue is widely recognised as one of the UK's foremost movement directors, working on major stages both at home: The Royal National Theatre, The Royal Court Theatre, Glyndebourne, and fifteen years at the Royal Shakespeare Company, and abroad including: the Vienna State Opera, Opera Comique, Paris, The Metropolitan Opera, New York. Film credits as a movement director include: *Elizabeth,* with Kate Blanchett, *Pride and Prejudice*, with Gwyneth Paltrow and *The Libertine*, with Johnny Depp. Sue is co-artistic director with Sonja Linden of Visible Theatre Ensemble.

Norma Cohen – actor

Liverpool-born and Laban movement/dance trained, Norma worked with radical/experimental theatre companies based at Ovalhouse in the 70s/80s. As writer/performer, she founded Ship of Fools, touring *Oy Vey,*

Fung Shway, Sympathetic Magic (King's Head), *Does it Come with Ketchup?* (Rosemary Branch). Theatre includes: Hazel in *DUSK* (Catherine Willmore, Epping Forest), Pushkin's *The Queen of Spades* (Max Hoehn, Arcola), Rozenmacher's *Requiem for a Friday Night* (Daniel Goldman, Venezuelan Embassy), *POP* (Trilby James, Tristan Bates), *9.21 to Shrub Hill* (New Diorama), Willy Russell's *One for the Road* (Century), John Burrows' *The Last Cabaret* (Albany Empire) *& Son of a Gun* (ICA/ Sidewalk), Ken Campbell's *School for Clowns* (Liverpool Everyman), *A Nuclear Cabaret* (Cunning Stunts, Tricycle), Rose Tremain's *Yoga Class* (Monstrous Regiment), Shane Connaughton's *Sir is Winning* (Pirate Jenny), Peter Flannery's *The Last Resort* (John Caird), *The Exception and the Rule* (John Dove). Upcoming: film: *The Fitzroy* (Andrew Harmer, Dresden Pictures), *Marriage* (Katerina Curtis, Inventome Films); upcoming theatre: writer/ performer: *On the Brink* (Rosemary Branch, 2015).

Jasmina Daniel – actor

Anglo-Iranian Jasmina trained at LAMDA and worked extensively in theatre, television and film for 15 years, prior to working overseas as an actor, as a University lecturer in Taiwan and Grenada and as a Scuba diving instructor in Australia, Germany, Kenya and Martinique. In 1980, Jasmina was on the RGS Expedition to Pitcairn, later joining Operation Raleigh in Australia and Guyana. Now back in the UK, her recent theatre work includes *The Last of the Duchess* (Richard Eyre, Hampstead), *The House of Bernarda Alba* (Bijan Sheibani, Almeida), *Pera Palas* (Arcola) and many productions for the German company Interkultur. Also included are *The Chair Women* (Riverside Studios), *As Time Goes By* (Fiddler's Elbow), *Crocodile Seeking Refuge* (Ice and Fire), *Hard Places* (Colchester and India) and a reading of *Scorched* (Braham

Murray, Old Vic). Next January Jasmina will be in fellow Visible Norma's play *On the Brink* in London.

Trevor Allan Davies – actor

Canadian born, Trevor has worked as an actor, director, writer and musician in the UK and Canada. Since immigrating to Britain in 1976, he has appeared in many fringe, repertory and West End productions, and in film, television and radio. Work includes: *Rosencrantz and Guildenstern are Dead* (Trevor Nunn, Chichester Festival and Theatre Royal Haymarket), *Women Beware Women* (Lawrence Boswell, RSC), *The Three Sisters* (Mike Alfreds, Shared Experience), and *KickAss2* (feature film). Most recently he appeared as Fennesz in *Game of Thrones*. He has taught the Alexander Technique in the UK, Canada and the USA since he completed training in 1991. He and his wife now grow and sell organic seasonal cut flowers in Hertfordshire and Buckinghamshire through their new company Gillyflower.

Ann Firbank – actor

Brought up in India until the age of 12, Annie later trained at Old Vic Theatre School and RADA. She has worked extensively in nearly all the major theatres in the UK, most recently in *The Crucible* (Yael Farber, Old Vic), *To Kill A Mockingbird* (Max Webster, Manchester Royal Exchange), *The Golden Dragon* (Ramin Gray, ACT) and in five previous ACT productions directed by Nick Philippou. Other work includes: *Three Sisters, An Ideal Husband, Separate Tables, Habitat* (Manchester Royal Exchange), *Macbeth* (John Caird, Almeida), *Becket* (John Caird, Haymarket). For the RSC: *The Hollow Crown, Comedy of Errors, Henry V* (directed by Ed Hall), *Much Ado About Nothing* (Declan Donnellan , Cheek by Jowl), *A Handful of Dust* (Mike Alfreds, Shared Experience). *The*

Passion (Bill Bryden, National Theatre), Julius Caesar (John Schlesinger, National Theatre), Mary Stuart (Nicki Kay, BAC), High Society (Richard Eyre, Victoria Palace), A Doll's House (Royal Lyceum Theatre, Edinburgh). Annie works frequently with Wonderful Beast (director Alys Kihl), a company committed to myths, legends and fairy tales.

Imola Gaspar – actor

Imola is a Romanian (Transylvanian) born Hungarian actress. After she graduated from the Academy of Drama and Film, she went on to have an extensive film and theatre career. She played at the National Theatre of Romania before moving to Hungary in 1993 to work at the National Theatre of Hungary. She has worked with leading directors such as Romanian Viktor Frunza, Polish Andrzey Wajda and Hungarian Istvan Szabo. Her previous work includes *Hamlet* (Frunza, National Theatre Romania), *Man for All Seasons, Tartuffe, The Wedding* (Wajda, National Theatre Hungary), *One Hundred Years of Solitude* (National Theatre Romania), *Blood Wedding* (National Theatre Romania), *Love and Intrigue*. She performed in over 40 film roles in Europe and America Recent work includes one of the lead roles in the American feature film *Action Words: Stand of Faith* directed by Darwin Brooks. She has won 3 awards for best actor in Hungary, Romania and Portugal. Imola has been in the UK since 2008. http://www.imolagaspar.com/

Andrew Hawkins – actor

London-born Andrew Hawkins acted in the British premieres of *Red Cross* and *Chicago* by Sam Shepard. He went on to work in repertory at Bristol, Colchester, Ipswich, Edinburgh and Birmingham. Work with the RSC: *Baal, The Suicide, Pericles,* and *Nicholas Nickleby* at the Aldwych and on Broadway; *I Have Before Me a Remarkable Document...* by Sonja Linden (Finborough), *Time and the Conways* (The Old Vic and Toronto), *The Clandestine Marriage* at the Albery; *The Cenci* (Lyric Hammersmith); *Wedding Story* (Soho Theatre); *King Lear* (Manchester Royal Exchange). In 2010, he performed his own show *Naked, Live... and Never Again* at the Pleasance, Edinburgh. Film credits include *Chariots of Fire, The Object of Beauty* and *Shadowlands*. TV includes *Foyle's War, Midsomer Murders* and the *The Trial of the King Killers*. With Agnes Treplin he collaborated in a performance work *Flight,* at the National Gallery (live) and in *Out of Our Heads* at Shoreditch Town Hall (film).

Paul Humpoletz – actor

Born in the UK of an Austrian father and Hungarian mother, Paul has worked in many regional theatres throughout the United Kingdom, as well as London and the West End. Previous work includes: *Romeo and Juliet* (Terry Hands, Theatre Clwd), *The Tempest* (Silviu Purcarete, Nottingham Playhouse and World Tour), *A Doll's House* (Annie Castledine, Chichester), *Dracula* (Brigid Lamour, Manchester Contact Theatre), *Present Laughter* (Janice Dunn, Mercury Theatre), *Sweeny Todd* (Donald Sartain, Dundee), plus many productions for the German-based company, *Interkultur*. Amongst his many TV roles he played Winston Churchill in an acclaimed performance in *World War Two: Behind Closed Doors* for BBC2. He has appeared in numerous feature films and BBC radio dramas, and given many poetry recitals. He has recently been touring *The Edge of Tranquility,* his one-man show based on the life of Handel.

Togo Igawa – actor

Born in Tokyo, Togo was an active member of the Black Tent Theatre for 13 years touring 120 cities all over Japan.

He moved to the UK in 1983, and was the first Japanese actor with the RSC in the opening season of the Swan Theatre. Previous work includes: *The Face of Jizo* (Togo directed, Arcola), *Pacific Overtures* (Garry Griffin, Donmar Warehouse), *The Ashgirl* (Lucy Bailey, Birmingham Rep), *The Great Highway* (David Farr, Gate), *The Great White Hope* (Nicholas Kent, RSC), *The Fair Maid of the West* (Trevor Nunn, RSC), *The Rover* (John Barton, RSC), *Abe Sada's Dog* (Makoto Satoh, BTT). Films including *Hector and the Search for Happiness* (Peter Chelsom), *Street Fighter: Assassin's Fist* (Joey Ansah), *47 Ronin* (Carl Rinsch), *Johnny English Reborn* (Oliver Parker), *The Hedgehog* (Mona Achache), John Rabe (Florian Gallenberger), *Speed Racer* (The Wachowski Brothers), *The Last Samurai* (Edward Zwick), *Code 46* (Michael Winterbottom), *Eyes Wide Shut* (Stanley Kubrick), *Topsy-Turvy* (Mike Leigh) and *The Tribe* (Stephen Poliakoff).

John Moraitis – actor

Born in New York City of Greek parentage, John trained at the Actors Studio. Recent work includes the title role in *King Lear* (UK/Ireland/Vietnam/Japan/China tours). Previous work includes *Six Degrees of Separation* (Old Vic), Willy Loman in *Death of a Salesman*, (European tour), *A View From The Bridge* (West End/UK tour and Theatre Clywd), *Welcome to Ramallah* (Arcola), *Fragile* (Arcola), *Crocodile Seeking Refuge* (UK tour) *True West* (Duke's Lancaster), *Julius Caesar* (Caesar), *Deathtrap, The Merchant of Venice* (Shylock). USA work includes: *An Enemy of the People, One Flew Over The Cuckoo's Nest, The Fire Raisers, Losing Venice, A Christmas Carol, The Trial, The Birds, Breakfast at Tiffany's, The Good Woman of Szechuan*. Television includes *New Tricks, The Misfits, Genie in the House, Murder in Paradise, NY-LON, First Degree, Office Gossip, People Like Us,*

Law and Order, NYPD Blue, As the World Turns. Film includes *Woman in Gold* (2015 release), *God the Father, The Fifth Estate, A Bunch of Amateurs, United 93, Where the Truth Lies, London Book of the Dead, Booty Call* and *Goodfellas.*

Ruth Posner – actor

Born in Poland, Ruth was a child survivor of the Warsaw Ghetto. She has lived in the UK since her teens and originally trained as a dancer, becoming an original member of London Contemporary Dance Co. During her 9 years in New York, Ruth studied with Uta Hagan, obtained an MA in Theatre Arts from Hunter College and taught movement at The Juilliard School, NY and Brandeis College in Boston. Theatre credits include: *Seven Jewish Children* (Dominic Cooke, Royal Court), *Dybbuk* (Katie Mitchell, RSC) *Merchant of Venice* (Julia Pascal Arcola, RSC), *Hiawatha* (Susan Todd, Bristol Old Vic), *Ritual in Blood* (Steven Berkoff, Nottingham Playhouse), *Blood Wedding* (Tim Supple, Young Vic), *Yiddish Queen Lear* (written for her and directed by Julia Pascal) as well as *Theresa* (written for her by Julia Pascal), which toured France and Germany. She was *Mother Millennium* at the Dome and has done 6 plays for BBC Radio and several other television performances for BBC TV and BBC Wales. Recent film work: a new comedy for BBC TV, *Count Arthur Strong* directed by Graham Lineham.

Adah Kay – Executive Director

British born to Russian parents, Adah Kay trained as a social anthropologist and urban planner. Her career has spanned academic teaching, research and evaluation, work in local authorities and in the non-profit/charity sector. She recently retired as Visiting Professor at the Cass Business School, the City University, where she helped establish the Centre for Charity Effectiveness. Adah now focuses on research and writing on human rights issues. Her interest in working in theatre was sparked off by her first play, *Welcome to Ramallah* co-written with Sonja Linden and produced at the Arcola by iceandfire theatre in 2008.

Lynne Hale – Assistant Executive Director

Lynne grew up in Wales but spent the early part of her career in the US, teaching English Language at New York and Harvard Universities and studying theatre. Returning to the UK she continued university teaching, then moved onto the non-profit/charity sector. As a former Executive Director of Haringey Shed, a small inclusive theatre charity, Lynne has extensive experience of fundraising, strategic development, governance and people management. Working with Visible allows her to draw together many strands of her interests and experience.

VISIBLE TRUSTEES

Roger Winfield

David Metz

Tish Francis

Emily Gottlieb

CREATIVE TEAM

Agnes Treplin – Designer

Agnes was born in Germany and has worked on many productions for opera, dance, theatre, musicals and film in the UK and internationally. Her most recent design credits: *A Dashing Fellow* (New Diorama Theatre, London) *Werther. Die Sprache der Liebe, Am Horizont*

(Hans Otto Theater, Potsdam, Germany), *Warsaw Melody* (Arcola Theatre, London), *Consultants* and *Man in the Middle* (Theatre 503, London) *Land of The Gypsies* (Grand Theatre, Lebanon) *The Marriage of Figaro* and *Don Pasquale* (ETO) *The Rise of the Phoenix , Gibran The Prophet* and *Don Quixote* for the Byblos International Festival, Lebanon, Al Mutanabbi (Baalbek Festival, Lebanon), *Der Freischuetz* (National Theatre of Iceland), *Othello* (Basingstoke Theatre). She is currently course director for the MA Costume Design for Performance at London College of Fashion and has recently made the costume film *Flight* shown at the *Out Of Our Heads* exhibition at Shoreditch Town Hall. She is currently designing *The 39 Steps* for the English Theatre Vienna.

Neill Brinkworth – Lighting Designer

Born in Bristol, Neill Brinkworth was involved in *Dessa Rose* (Trafalgar Studios); *Lambeth* (Southwark Playhouse); *The Night Garden Live* (Minor/BBC); *Lohengrin* (Warsaw National Opera, Associate); *Symbionts* (Wayne McGregor/Estonia National Ballet, Associate); *Café Chaos* (The Kosh); *Dido & Aeneas* (English Touring Opera); *The Seagull* (Arcola); *An Enemy of the People* (Albany); *Jephthe* (ETO); *Strauss Gala* (Raymond Gubbay); *Bridgetower* (City of London/ETO); *Ludd & Isis* (Royal Opera House, Associate); *Vincent River* (Old Vic productions); *Step 9 of 12; Tape* (Trafalgar Studios); *Maria Stuarda* (Opera North, associate); *Variete; Burnt Out Souls* (YMT UK); *Rooms, a rock romance* (Finborough); *The Tin Soldier (peut etre); Dick Whittington* (Hertford Theatre); *Lean* (Tristan Bates); *Prometheus/The Frogs/Agamemnon* (Cambridge Arts Theatre); *Accolade; Fanta Orange; Don Juan Comes Back from the War* (Finborough Theatre); *Seven Pomegranate Seeds* (Oxford Playhouse); *Six Men & A Poker Game* (Gridiron); *A Square of Sky* (The Kosh).

Gillian Tan – Projections Designer

Singapore born Gillian is a Visual Engineer and Specialist Producer, exploring the use of projection and video in the entertainment industry through the development of new technologies, as well as challenging the boundaries of audience experiences in live events and theatre. Recent credits include: Video Designer for the Royal Exchange Theatre and PINGNG Productions' *Crocodiles*, Associate Video Designer for Wizard Production's *I Believe in Unicorns* at the Vaudeville Theatre (West End), Video Engineer for Secret Cinema's *Back to the Future* and Digital Engineer for Brolly Production's workshop of *Clocks*, the steampunk opera. She hails from the sunny island of Singapore, and is eternally grateful to Tim Bird and Lucy Ockenden for introducing her to the world of video and to Visible for giving her this opportunity.

Andy Taylor – Sound Designer

Born and bred in North London (Tottenham and Hendon) Andy graduated with a Music degree from Huddersfield University in 1990 having spent far too much time playing with the sound-studio technology in between practicing the piano and composing. He then worked in various music recording studios (including CTS, Lansdowne, Strongroom, Whitfield Street and Abbey Road) recording a variety of film and TV scores with composers such as Hans Zimmer, Trevor Jones and Alan Silvestri; and albums with artists such as Stan Tracey, Tina May, Anthony Newley and Shirley Bassey. To see the sun again he then moved into teaching where he taught Sound and Music Technology to a wide variety of students. He achieved his PGCE in 1999 and his MA (Audio Technology) in 2007. He now teaches Sound Technology and Sound Design at the Guildhall School of Music & Drama.

Sally Davies – Music Director/Composer

Brought up in England and in the Pezalozzi international children's village in Switzerland, Sally trained at Dartington College and went on to work as a dancer, actor and musician within the theatre, touring extensively in Britain and Europe. In the mid 90s she studied for and gained an MA in composition and ethnomusicology. Primarily a musician for the last couple of decades, she is a composer, music director, multi-instrumentalist and singer. She has undertaken numerous music commissions for dance and theatre companies such as Green Candle, and her music has been performed in diverse venues from Sadlers Wells to the Edinburgh Festival, from the Purcell Room to the Festival of Polyphonic Singing in Tblisi. She directs two *a cappella* choirs – the folk choir at Cecil Sharp House and the Wing-It Singers who specialise in songs from Eastern Europe. She performs regularly as one half of the duo, Bow and Bellows.

Francesca Ter-Berg – Cellist

Francesca Ter-Berg, is one of the leading Klezmer cellists of her generation. Growing up in East London, she was surrounded by many different cultures which influenced her decision to study Social Anthropology at the University of Sussex. After graduating in 2007 she began to pursue her passion for traditional and roots music and commenced her travels through Europe and North America to study with prominent experts in Klezmer and Romany music including Dr Alan Bern, Frank London and Tcha Limberger. Since returning to London Francesca has continued to explore the traditions on her doorstep such as Middle Eastern and Indian Classical music. She has collaborated with many of London's top artists including acclaimed folk singers Sam Lee, Katy Carr and Lisa Knapp, the BBC Symphony Orchestra, Riz MC and

Tabla player and producer Talvin Singh. She is featured on Sam Lee's Mercury Prize nominated album 'A Ground of it's Own' and was Musical Director for Katy's Carr's latest release 'Paszport' which received 4/5 star reviews. Francesca lives in London and in her spare time runs the pop-up restaurant World Brunch Club.

Michael Ager – Production Manager

Michael is a Freelance Theatre Production Manager, born and raised in Romford, Essex. He previously worked at the Young Vic Theatre as Technician and Production Manager for the Taking Part Department (2007 – 2013) where he production-managed numerous projects with Young People, Schools, Local Community and Young Directors in the Clare and Maria Theatres. Recent productions include: *Flat Stanley* (Engine House Productions); *The Edge of our Bodies* (The Gate); *The Saints* and *The Best Christmas Present in the World* (Nuffield Playing Field); *In Lambeth* (Spell Bound Productions); *Debris* (Open Works); *London Wall* and *What The Women Did* (Two's Company Productions); *Tutto Bene Mama, The Last Yankee* and *Ignis* (The Print Room); *Donny's Brain, Godchild, Fault Lines, The Blackest Black* and *In The Vale of Health* (Hampstead Theatre); *Early Days* (Of a Better Nation) (for Coney at Battersea Arts Centre, Warwick Arts Centre & Frascati Theater Amsterdam).

Naomi Hill – Stage Manager

Born and raised in South Leicestershire Naomi has been working in theatre for the past 13 years. Recent theatre credits include *South Pacific, Sister Act,* and *My Fair Lady* for Kilworth House Theatre, national tour of *Moon on a Rainbow Shawl* for Talawa Theatre Company/ National Theatre, *God's Property* at the Soho Theatre for Talawa Theatre Company, *Gotta Sing Gotta Dance* for

Eastbourne Theatres, national tour of *Why I Don't Hate White People* with Lemm Sissay, *Blonde Bombshells of 1943* national and Far East tour. She has also worked on over 10 pantomimes and is looking forward to touring again with Talawa Theatre Company on their production of *All My Sons* in the new year.

Liam Borrett – Assistant Director

Originally from Norfolk, Liam moved to London to train as a director at Drama Centre London. It was there that he developed an interest in writing, which led to the creation of his first play, *This Is Living*. Liam directed the piece for the Edinburgh Fringe Festival this year, playing at Bedlam Theatre, where it won EntertainmentWise's Best New Play award. As Assistant Director, Liam has worked at Theatre 503, (Thatcherwrite Festival), RichMix/Tristan Bates Theatre *Hannah 27 : Adventures in Online Dating* Pleasance Courtyard *Family Tree* and the Platform Theatre *The White Guard*. A section of Liam's second play *Possessions* will be performed as part of Miniaturists 49 at the Arcola Theatre this November. Liam is Artistic Director of new playwriting theatre company, Falling Through Water. http://www.fallingthroughwater.com/

Meg Kubota – actor (voiceover for Yoko)

Meg is originally from Japan but has been living in the UK for a long time. Her theatre credits include *Hanjo* (Oval House); *The Girl Named Shining Brightly* (Polka Children's Theatre); *Festival For the Fish* (Wimbledon Theatre). Her Film & TV credits include: *Iris* (Fox Iris Prduction); *Fog Bound* (Intermedia Films); *The Day of the Kamikaze* (Channel 4); *The Girl in a Bubble* (Actual Film); *The Followed* (Ether Films); *All That Remains* (Major Oak Entertainment). She is also known for her voice work in *Chuggington* (Cbeebies) as Dr Ling and more recently in *Mr Bean* the Animation due to be broadcast in 2015. On radio she played the lead in *A Pale View of the Hills* and *Fewer Not Less* (Radio 4), and a number of other radio dramas. She is also a qualified yoga teacher.

PRODUCTION TEAM

Claire French – Associate Producer

Australian born to Irish and British parents, Claire is a theatre-maker and researcher who has most extensively worked as producer in Australia and Germany. Training first at the Western Australian Academy of Performing Arts (WAAPA), Claire directed and produced productions independently, including *Platform* (Patricia Cornelius, Fly by Night Musicians Club) and *Presence* (Patrick van der Werf, state tour, Subiaco Arts Centre). As festival director of Perth's open-air amphitheatre 'bamBOO' she programmed and produced three years of six-monthly interdisciplinary arts festivals including theatre, dance and cinema. This included the three-year run of *Eat my Monologue* featuring work by Andrew Bovell, Tom Holloway and Damian Millar. This led Claire to Berlin, Germany to garner new approaches to her practice, also seeing her work in the international film festival industry. Most recently completing an MA at the Royal Central School of Speech and Drama, London, Claire's current practice interests are testimonial and documentary theatre. Recent shows include *Housed* (David Watson, Old Vic Community Company); *The War Party* (Fulham Palace, Museums at Night); and, work with participatory video NGO InsightShare, Oxford.

Sophia Klose – Assistant Producer

Born in Berlin, Germany, Sophia moved to London in 2012 to attend the BA Drama, Applied Theatre & Education course at the Royal Central School of Speech & Drama. She has focused on playwriting and graduated with a First Class degree in July 2014. Being a co-founder of Nova X Press, she has been illustrating and creating original books in collaboration with the award-winning British poet and novelist Jeremy Reed. Since August 2014, Sophia has been working as an intern with Visible Ensemble. http://novaxpress.co.uk/

Production Photography – John Haynes

Press Photography – Nadia Otshodi

Writer with the Company – Sonja Linden.

This text went to press before the end of rehearsals and so may differ slightly from the play as performed.

BackstageTrust

Scene List

PART 3.

Mostly though not entirely in 1950s

26. RABBITS. Tokyo 1952.

27. SOAP-BOX EVE. Colindale 1956.

28. DISGRACE. Tokyo/London 1950s.

29. LOVE AND WAR Transylvania 1950s.

30. SKYPE 2. London/Tokyo 2014/1945.

INTERVAL

PART 4:

Revolutionary times: the 1960s, 70s, and 80s

31. IF YOU REMEMBER IT, YOU WEREN'T THERE. 1960s.

32. WHERE IS ANNA LAGANA? Italy 1969.

33. THE BRITISH ROAD TO SOCIALISM. Merseyside Docks 1960s.

34. KOMMUNIZMUS. England/Bucharest 1960s, 70s.

35. THE DRAFT. New York 1972.

36. FLIGHT 1978.

37. THE BIRTHDAY SPEECH. Romania 1989.

PART 5:

"Ripeness is all" Mostly the 21st Century.

38. ENDGAME: Wiener Library, London 2006.

39. ENDGAME: Singapore, 1993.

40. LEAR IN VIETNAM Ho Chi Minh City 2012.

41. All RIGHT, DEAR? Royal Free Hospital, London 2014.

EPILOGUE

PRODUCTION NOTE:

Section and scene titles are projected onto a screen, as are occasional images, largely photographs from the actors' family archives.

WHO DO WE THINK WE ARE?

by Sonja Linden and Company

The play was premiered on 29th October at Southwark Playhouse, London. Directed by Sue Lefton.

CHARACTERS

John

Norma

Annie

Ruth

Andrew

Jasmina

Togo

Imola

Paul

Trevor

Togo's wife

Aunt Stamatoula – John's aunt

Family members from the Greek island of Ikaria

George – Trevor's grandfather

Blod – Trevor's grandmother

Dancing soldier

Humpo – Pauls' father

Emil, Otto, Austrian officers

Sergei – Russian Guard

Red Guard Commissar

Humpo's Viennese mother

Klaus – Austrian officer

Jasmina's Persian Grandmother

Karim, Abdul, Hamid, – Persian grandmother's 3 young sons

Madiheh, Persian maid

Ruth aged 9 - 13 yrs

Ruth's father

Ruth's mother

Annie aged 9-10 yrs

Morrie - London greengrocer

London policeman

Nazi female guard

Ruth's aunt

Jack Hawkins – Andrew's father

Doreen Lawrence – Andrew's mother

Major, Colonel, Brigadier – army officers posted in India in World War Two

Harry Pollitt

Eve – Norma's mother

Igawa-san – Togo's father

Matild – Imola's aunt

Janos
Andrew aged 18
Stefano's mother
Stefano's cook
Sicilan slum dwellers
Italian café patrons
Norma, in her teens
Imola, in her teens
Edit – Imola's friend
Romanian crowd
John aged 21

Dr Fisher – American psychiatrist
Giant Manta Ray
Romanian theatre director
Singapore hospital patients and visitors
Vietnamese teenagers
Vietnamese teacher
Vietnamese Buddist monk
British Nurse
British Doctor

PROLOGUE

JOHN   I remember...

NORMA   I remember so much

ANNIE   I remember so little...

JOHN   The look on her face

RUTH   Her face, and the feel of his fingers

ANDREW   ... her fingers, the smell of her scent...

JASMINA   I remember his voice...

ANNIE   ... his voice fading now

NORMA   I remember her saying...

TOGO   I think I remember her saying

Beat.

IMOLA   I remember...

ANDREW I remember my parents telling me...

IMOLA   Mine too

PAUL   ... when they showed me the photos in the family album

Beat.

IMOLA   I remember,

TREVOR   Though maybe I've added...

RUTH   Or removed from my mind, taken away

JASMINA From what really happened – who knows...

TREVOR   Who knows what happened, really happened? We think...

PAUL   We think it went something like...

JOHN   Something like this, but then again...

TOGO   DID IT?

PAUL   Who can know for sure how much of it is true?

JOHN   Truth or Lies?

ANNIE   Or Lies or half-truths, half- remembered?

PART 1

Mostly though not entirely around the time of the First World War

1. SKYPE. Banbury/Tokyo 2014

Togo, Narrator, Togo's wife, Yoko (Voice of Togo's sister).

Togo's living room in Banbury, Oxfordshire. Togo enters stage right carrying a laptop. He crosses the stage and sets it up on a table, under the following voiceover. Narrator enters stage left and observes him, then delivers the translation of Yoko's voiceover.

YOKO ある日、男は聞こうと思った。

[Aruhi nêsan-ni kikôto omotta otokogairu]

NARRATOR One day a man decides to ask a question.

YOKO いままで聞いたことのない質問。

[Imamade kiitakotononai shitsumon]

NARRATOR A question that he has not thought to ask before.

YOKO 答えられるのは、家族の中でたったひとり生き残っている人。

[Kotaerarerunowa kazokuno nakade tatta hitori ikinokotteiru hito]

NARRATOR And now there's only one person in the family still alive who can give him the answer...

YOKO 姉の洋子。

[Aneno Yôko]

NARRATOR His sister Yoko.

TOGO   That man is me. *(stands and bows)*

Enter Togo's English wife, wearing a potter's apron, and carrying a sake flask. She sits on a chair next to him, ready to join in the Skype.

YOKO   役者で、夫で、父親で、洋子の弟。

   [Yakushade, ottode, chichioyade, Yôko no otôto]

NARRATOR Actor. Husband. Father. Brother of Yoko.

We hear the sound of a Skype call being made. On the screen we now see a small image of Togo's face in the corner of the screen and a Skype logo silhouette for his sister as the Skype call begins.

TOGO   もしもし、洋子？聞こえる？

   [Moshimoshi, Yôko? Kikoeru?]

2. QUESTION. Ikaria 2014

Narrators, John, his aunt.

Seagull sounds.

NARRATOR 1 On another day, in another place and at another time, a different man decides to ask a question.

NARRATOR 2 Not from his sister but from his father's sister.

NARRATOR 3 It's a question that has occurred to him before.

NARRATOR 1 But which he hasn't asked till now.

NARRATOR 3 Why?

NARRATOR 2 Perhaps because he doesn't get to see his aunt that often.

NARRATOR 1 Or, perhaps it's just because he's getting older and he senses his own mortality.

NARRATOR 3 Or hers! She's 99 years old.

NARRATOR 2 That's nothing where she comes from, on the Greek Island of Ikaria...

NARRATOR 1 ... people live to be a hundred and still go about their business of farming or fishing.

NARRATOR 3 Maybe he's come to find the secret of longevity.

JOHN *(to his aunt)* Thea Stamatoula? Fenese kalla.

NARRATOR 2 Aunt Stamatoula? You're looking well.

His aunt nods in reply.

JOHN Eethela na se aroteeso kati gia ton patera mou, o adelfos sou.

NARRATOR 2 I've been meaning to ask you something about my father, your brother.

JOHN *(to the narrators)* I couldn't exactly ask him myself – he died when I was only two. *(to his aunt)* Kserees pios eeime, etsi then eeine?

NARRATOR 2 You know who I am, right?

Aunt smiles and pulls out a baseball cap and waves it at John under the next speech.

JOHN My God, you've still got that! *(unable to fit his head into it)* My head's grown a bit since I was 10. *(to narrators)* I heard she talked to it after I went back to the States. She missed me. I reminded her of my father, the brother who went away. *(to aunt)* I wanted to ask you... *(Aunt beckons for him to speak up.)* I wanted to ask you about the day my Dad left the island. I don't even know exactly what year that was. Do you know? *(bending an ear to his aunt's lips then relaying her answer to everyone, surprised)* 1914!

The company break into a 1914 ragtime dance which segues into the next scene.

3. IT'S 1914 AND...

Andrew, Imola, Jasmina, Togo, Norma.

ANDREW 1914 and my grandfather Horace is trying to break into the acting profession in the southern counties of England. Two year later though, and he will find himself in the battle of the Somme, fighting in the ranks of the Hampshire Regiment, 2nd Battalion. He'll be lucky to survive, and probably even luckier still to get pneumonia, which will get him out of the freezing trenches and back to hospital in Southampton, where he will meet my grandmother, working there as a nurse.

IMOLA   1914 and my grandfather, Béla, leaves his village in Transylvania in Hungary to serve in the Austro-Hungarian army. He will fight the Italians in the famous battle of Doberdo, a very bloody battle with hand-to-hand fighting. 20,000 will die. The Italians win.

JASMINA 1914 and my English grandfather is a captain in the Royal Fusiliers. Three years later he will find himself lying in a ditch filled with corpses somewhere on the Western Front. When they try to pull him out, his arm drops off – gangrene. He's patched up and sent back into battle only to be shot in the lung. Strapped for time the doctor decides it's quicker to remove the whole lung, bullet an' all. Cuts him open – can't find the other one. "Oh dear, better leave that lung in then." Stitches him up again and my grandfather – later to become Colonel Sir Eric Norman Spencer Crankshaw K.C.M.G. – lives on with one arm and one lung for another 50 years. Good old Crankie.

TOGO   1914 and my uncle has been exempted from military service as a medical student. Four years later he will be sent as a doctor to Siberia with the Japanese army, who are fighting on the side of the allies. My uncle is surprised to find his first patients are women – Japanese prostitutes sent by the government to service the soldiers. They don't want their soldiers to catch venereal diseases from the local Siberian women. Now my uncle understands why he's been sent there. He's a gynaecologist.

NORMA   1914, and my father Eric is part of the crowd watching King George and Queen Mary see the troops off in Liverpool. My Russian Jewish Liverpudlian grandfather proudly takes a photograph. There's a lot of waving and cheering and people singing God Save the King. My Dad, who is to become a life long member of the communist party, doesn't join in – or so he says. He's only four, but already he's going against the stream!

JASMINA 1914, and my Persian father Abdul Hossein, is playing in the rose filled gardens of his family compound in Teheran, unaware that his country will soon be occupied by the Russians, the French and the British. He's also four years old.

4. DISPATCHED. Vienna 1914

The whole company are strolling through the Prater Park, Vienna. Live accordion music plays.

PAUL 1914, and my father Paul Humpoletz is strolling through the Prater Park in Vienna...

NARRATOR 1 ... It's a Saint's Day in Austria, June 28th to be precise.

PAUL And the park is filled with holidaymakers.

NARRATOR 2 It's a gorgeous day, a band is playing and all is well with the world when suddenly the music stops...

NARRATOR 2 A notice is put up on the bandstand. The musicians start to pack up their instruments.

A whisper passes through the group using the following words 'Kronprinz', 'umgrebracht', 'erschossen', 'Sarajevo'.

NARRATOR 3 *(shocked, to the crowd)* Der Kronprinz ist umgebracht! Von einem Serben erschossen, in Sarajevo, mit seiner Frau.

PAUL And that's when my father – a captain in the Austro-Hungarian army – learns about the assassination of the Emperor's nephew in Sarajevo.

NARRATOR 4 One month later to the very day, Austria declares war on Serbia, then on Russia.

PAUL And my father is dispatched to the Russian front.

Slow fade on Paul who as his father packs up his army things, puts on his greatcoat and hoists his army bag onto his shoulders under the following scene.

5. FAREWELLS. Ikaria 1914

John, the company, narrators.

Seagull sounds.

JOHN   The day my father left his little island in the Aegean sea, the whole family came down to the shore to see him off.

The actors become the family and enact the departure. His mother hands him a cardboard suitcase and an old-fashioned cap.

NARRATOR 1 Including your great grandfather, the village priest...

NARRATOR 2 ... with his enormous beard. *(looking at the photo projection of his grandfather)* And big cherubic smile.

We hear goodbyes in Greek, half-spoken, half sung: Otheos masisu [God be with you]; Yasu [goodbye]; Kalo taksidi.

JOHN   As the boat pulls away the smells of the island still cling to his nostrils.

NARRATOR 3 He looks back at the white-painted houses gleaming in the sun.

JOHN   At the huddled figures on the shore, growing ever smaller.

More goodbyes in Greek. John waves, the crowd waves back.

JOHN   Only the oarsman can see how wet are his eyes, for till now he has withheld his tears to protect his weeping mother. It's a sacrifice for him, for his parents, to leave everything behind for America, to earn money for the family. He's 13 years old.

John as his father Gyorgi with his suitcase and Paul as his father Captain Humpoletz with his army rucksack, cross over as they each head in opposite directions. Trevor as his grandfather George emerges from the crowd putting on the uniform jacket and hat of a Canadian soldier in the Royal Winnipeg Rifles, in the first world war. He is carrying a soldier's backpack.

Blod steps forward to join Trevor and they become Trevor's grand-parents, Blod and George

Lights down on the remaining actors.

6. DEPARTURE. Winnipeg 1915

Trevor, George (Trevor), Blod.

TREVOR My Canadian grandfather has signed up for the war, leaving behind his young wife Blodwyn, who is pregnant with my father. The first time my grandfather will see his son is in a photograph she sends him to the trenches in France. (*This postcard comes up on screen.*) But now he's headed for his troopship which sails from Nova Scotia to Liverpool.

The garden of his grandfather's house in Winnipeg.

GEORGE (*gently*) Now don't forget the garden.

BLOD (*touching her pregnant belly*) I can't do the garden darling.

GEORGE   All you need to know is what's a cabbage and what's a weed. All right?

BLOD   You got everything? Sandwiches?

GEORGE *(smiles)* I've got my sandwiches.

BLOD   Bible?

GEORGE   Got my bible.

BLOD   Shaving things? I got you a new shaving brush. Pure badger bristle.

GEORGE *(touched)* No need to do that girl.

BLOD   You'll think of me everyday now, when you shave with your new brush?

GEORGE   I will Blod. Write to me every week.

BLOD   I'll try. I will, I will.

GEORGE   Don't forget – cabbages and weeds. You'll be all right. And I'm gonna be all right. *(strong)* I'm coming back. Promise.

They kiss. George leaves. Blod remains standing in the garden, at a loss and remains there half lit during the next scene. An explosion of noise, of shells and gunfire leads into the next scene.

7. MUD AND DEATH. The Western Front 1916

Soldier, George, and company.

George is propelled by an explosive force into the middle of a field of mud.

The clamour of war is followed by a sudden almost shocking, utter silence.

A shell-shocked soldier appears. Discordant music under the soldier's dance.

GEORGE *(terrified, fearing it could be an enemy soldier)* Who's this? *(incredulous)* He's dancing! He's stopped. He's staring at me. My God, how can he still be alive? His face, it's just a gaping hole.

The dancing soldier collapses onto him. Music.

The ensemble are now gazing at him with distorted faces. A chorus of screams in unison.

GEORGE Where did that scream come from? (*Beat.*) It came from me.

Fragmented dance picking up from the dancing soldier's moves, after which the women go to their seats, as women left behind in war, and the men gather close around the stove in the next scene.

8. CAPTIVITY. Siberia 1918

Narrators, Austrian Officers: Humpo (Paul), Emil and Otto, Russian Guard Sergei, Bolshevik Commissar.

On screen Paul's father's P.O.W. photo with the duelling scars.

Lighting closes in creating an enclosed space. The sound of arctic wind and wolves howling. Humpo is sitting with a blanket over his shoulders, sketching. The other officers are engaged in different activities, trying to relieve their boredom by playing cards, reading, staring into space.

NARRATOR 1 Captain, now Colonel Humpoletz *(indicating P.O.W. photo with scars)* and his fellow Austrian officers are now in their fourth year as Russian prisoners-of-war in sub-zero Siberia.

NARRATOR 2 The Russians have pulled out of the war since the revolution, and the Bolshevik commissars are offering the POWs their freedom in return for fighting with them against the counter-revolutionary White Guards.

EMIL   So why aren't they fucking bringing us back home. *(pointing at Otto)* That's the fucking Hapsburgs for you.

OTTO   Language, please!

EMIL *(sarcastic)* Excuse me, I forgot you're a distant cousin a hundred times removed from the imperial family.

Stand-off between Emil and Otto.

HUMPO   Gentlemen, gentlemen, please.

Emil marches round the room getting more and more worked up.

OTTO   Anyway, if they brought us home now, they'd only send us to the Western Front. I'd rather sit the war out here.

EMIL *(at the window)* There's Sergei. *(calls out)* Hey Sergei. He's coming over. What do you bet me I can't get him to take us into the town again?

HUMPO   He won't do it for nothing.

OTTO   Offer to do a portrait of his wife.

HUMPO   I've already done one. Not sure it would go down too well though.

Otto starts scrabbling through some of Humpo's sketches.

OTTO   This it? *(finds the sketch which we then see on screen, a gross caricature)*

Laughter.

EMIL   Hide it! He's coming in.

The screen image disappears as if on cue.

OTTO *(lowering his voice)* Offer to do his tart then. That Verushka! Whooooah!

Sergei enters.

SERGEI   What is it now gentlemen?

EMIL   Fancy taking us into town, Comrade Guard, drinks on us?

SERGEI   You know the Reds have taken the town back again.

EMIL   So?

OTTO   What do you mean 'so'? The White Guards are far more well-disposed towards us.

SERGEI   Reds, Whites, shove them all out on the frozen tundra I say and let them all freeze to death, *(feeling Otto's greatcoat, which is slung over his shoulders)* You would be all right though. Nice bit of quality this. Warm as a pig's balls that must be. Not like this shit. Made from...

EMIL   ... yeah, yeah, stinging nettles, you told us a hundred times.

By now Sergei is standing over Humpo, looking at what he is sketching.

HUMPO *(touching his greatcoat, out of earshot of the others)* You want?

SERGEI   I want.

HUMPO   On one condition, when we get to the town... I might disappear *(touches his nose knowingly)*

EMIL   The Commissar's coming! Hey Otto fancy joining the Red Guards?

They shift their position. Enter Commissar.

COMMISSAR   Good evening, comrades

OFFICERS *(overlapping)* Good evening Comrade Commissar.

Lights go down on the actors who stay in position.

9. RETURN. Winnipeg 1918

George. 'Garden sounds'.

Lights up on George's garden. George has returned from the war and is approaching his house. He walks awkwardly, as though with some nervous disorder. He enters his garden then stops.

He surveys the garden then sinks to the ground and puts his hand in the soil. He is in a kind of reverie. We sense a change in him.

Lights down.

10. ESCAPE. Siberia 1918

Humpo (Paul), Humpo's Commissar, the company.

The screen title comes up as music starts and the lights come up on another part of the stage from George's garden.

We see Humpo, Emil, and the Commissar at the tavern drinking with Sergei. Amongst the women is Verushka who is serving and very flirtatious. Music, dancing and revelry are taking place. Humpo whispers to Emil to keep the Commissar's glass filled, while he makes a deal with Sergei. We see Sergei nervously swap his coat for Humpo's much more substantial greatcoat. Humpo then slips out of the door. Sergei sidles up to Verushka who has meanwhile been 'claimed' by the Commissar. Verushka catches sight of Humpo escaping, which alerts the Commissar. The other officer POWs and Sergei try to ply him with more vodka but he eventually breaks free and exits in a drunken stagger, pulling out his pistol and shooting it in the direction of Humpo.

Lights down sharply.

11. DUST TO DUST. Winnipeg 1918

George (Trevor), Blod.

Lights bang up instantly at sound of gunshot. We are back in George's garden.

At the sound of the gunshot, George flinches. This is followed by the tap-tap-tap of a woodpecker and his

realisation that it is a bird's cry that has startled him.
Blod emerges from the house and rushes towards him.

BLOD   Oh my God, oh my God, there you are.

GEORGE *(awkward)* Blod.

Blod embraces him and he puts his arms round her,
mechanically, finding this renewed intimacy difficult.

BLOD *(overcome with emotion)* George, George. We
were expecting you tomorrow. Look at you, you're so
skinny. Let me take this *(his bag)*.

GEORGE *(hugging the bag to him)* It's all right.

BLOD   George I can't believe you're here.

Avoiding making eye contact with her, he surveys
the garden.

BLOD *(indicating vegetable patch)* Look, isn't it good?
Isn't it lovely?

She watches George whose eyes are still fixed on
the garden.

BLOD   I bet you can't wait to see little Trevor. He
tells everyone you're a soldier, fought in the battle of
the Somme – proud as punch he is. You always wanted
a boy, didn't you, love?

George nods.

BLOD   Come inside now. *(indicating his bag)* Let
me take your bag for you.

GEORGE   No!

Their eyes lock for the first time.

BLOD *(tentative, reaches up to his cheek, as though to stroke it)* Tired is it, love? You've had a long journey.

No response.

BLOD   I'll go and get you some tea. *(exits)*

He watches her leave, then opens his bag and takes out a crumpled handkerchief. He digs a hole with his fingers in the patch of soil he's been scrabbling in, then tips the contents of the handkerchief into it, a handful of dusty, dry soil. He then covers it with garden soil as though he were burying something. Then he removes from his bag a small wooden cross and places it on this 'grave'.

GEORGE   I told you, you'd be coming home Arthur. Best I could do.

Lights fade down.

12. TRANS-SIBERIAN EXPRESS. Chita Station 1918

Humpo (Paul), Commissar (Togo), the company.

Lights fade up on Chita station and we discover Humpo pacing up and down the platform trying to keep warm, looking nervously around him all the time. Other passengers are waiting with suitcases. We hear the whistle of the arriving train. Everyone looks expectantly in its the direction. Suddenly the Commissar arrives, pistol in hand, looking drunk and dangerous. The other passengers shrink back, terrified, as is Humpo. We see the stationmaster, whistle at the ready, carrying a flag. We hear the sound of screeching brakes as the train arrives. We then hear the sound of train doors slamming followed by the train leaving. Finally only the frustrated Commissar is left on the platform.

Music to indicate time passing.

We see Humpo in a stylised light tramping through the snow as he continues his journey to Moscow, to be continued in parallel to the next scene. A sign marked Moscow in Cyrillic comes up on the screen.

13. BROKEN-HEARTED. Vienna 1918

Humpo's mother, Klaus.

The family Humpoletz's elegant Viennese apartment. Humpo's mother is seeing a man in uniform to the door, they shake hands, the man clearly feeling compassion for her.

MOTHER   You say he was brave?

KLAUS   He died with valour on the field, as a true officer of the imperial army. My deepest condolences Frau Humpoletz.

MOTHER   My husband will be broken-hearted.

KLAUS *(clicking his heels and kissing her hand)* Auf wiedersehen.

Klaus exits. Mother sits down and buries her face in her hands, where she remains half-lit during the next scene.

14. HOMECOMING. Teheran 1918

Jasmina, Grandmother (Jasmina), Narrator, Grandfather, the three young sons, Karim, Abdul, Hamid, Madiheh, the maid.

Lights come up on the palatial living room of the Hamzavi family in Teheran. An ornate French chair, and a large Persian rug on which sit the three sons of the family.

JASMINA At the same time, in another place, a different woman waits for news of a loved one – my grandmother.

Jasmina takes her place on the ornate chair and becomes her grandmother.

On screen an image of Jasmina's Persian grandfather fades up gradually under the next speech, becoming clear by the end of it.

GRANDMOTHER My husband is philosopher to Shah of Persia, and three years ago he disappeared.

NARRATOR No word has been heard from him in all that time, to the great distress of his wife and his three sons...

JASMINA *(smiling at him/patting his head)* The middle son, Abdul Hossein, being my father.

We see the three boys, Karim, Abdul, Hamid, looking disconsolate, and grandmother (Jasmina) sitting regally on her chair.

JASMINA Then one day, just after the first world war.

KARIM The maid came rushing in,

ABDUL Her long black hair flowing out behind her,

HAMID Tears streaming down her face.

MADIHEH The master's back! The master's back!

We see the boys' faces light up in excitement as they overlap:

KARIM   Papa is back!

ABDUL   Papa is back!

KARIM   Papa is back!

JASMINA Grandmama remains on her chair, very quiet and calm.

Music.

KARIM   But Papa doesn't appear.

NARRATOR Instead he goes down to his favourite rock in the garden and orders the ice with which he thinks great thoughts.

We see the grandfather thinking great thoughts, sucking on a piece of ice.

JASMINA Meanwhile the servants bring in camel bags...

KARIM   Carpet bags,

ABDUL   Rugs,

HAMID   Huge samovars,

JASMINA And lay this all out on a great pile of Persian rugs.

KARIM   Eventually grandfather comes in.

ABDUL   And the children are very quiet.

HAMID   Because he is a frightening man.

Grandmother remains composed, grandfather goes to her, then to the sons.

GRANDFATHER *(formal)* Greetings to you my sons. *(to the servants, clapping his hands)* And yes, now you may open the bags.

The sons open the bags enraptured, while grandmother looks on from her chair, trying to hide her curiosity and amazement and maintain her mask of dignity, under:

GRANDMOTHER There are silks, brocades, jewels of all colours...

KARIM   Rubies, emeralds,

ABDUL   Sapphires, diamonds,

HAMID   Necklaces, bracelets, rings,

GRANDMOTHER Uncut precious stones,

KARIM   Heaps of them tumbling out of the bags,

GRANDMOTHER Glittering in the candlelight.

MADIHEH *(lifting up a jeweled necklace to the light)* Even the smallest enough to live on for a year.

ABDUL   It's like Aladdin's cave!

JASMINA Evidently, the Shah had sent my grandfather to lead a group of men to quash some trouble on the border with Turkey. And so this – was pillage.

GRANDMOTHER *(Touching the necklace that Grandfather has put round her neck)* No doubt to win me over after his long absence.

Lights fade down, closing in on a final image of Grandfather standing behind Grandmother as lights and screen title fade up on Humpo and his mother in a similar position.

15. HOMECOMING. Vienna 1920

Humpo's mother, Humpo (Paul).

The Humpoletz's Vienna apartment.

MOTHER   Um Gottes Willen, dass kann nicht wahr sein!

HUMPO   Es ist wahr, Mutti.

MOTHER   Bist Du es wirklich Paul?

HUMPO   Ja, Mutti, ich bin es wirklich.

They embrace, his mother sobbing. Slow lighting fade broken by a sharp cruel light on George.

16. BANISHED. Winnipeg 1920

Trevor, George (Trevor), Blod.

We see George with a bundle of things in his arms, clothes and books, and most noticeably pyjamas, with Blod standing at a distance from him, arms folded resolute, both facing out.

TREVOR   My grandfather returned to Canada a broken man from his three years in the trenches.

George and Blod turn to face each other.

BLOD   He's immediately banished from the marital bed to a tiny bedroom in the attic.

TREVOR   He spends the next 25 years listening to the voices of his family through the floorboards.

Beat. Then we see them both, backs to each other, bent over, silently weeping.

17. CSARDAS. Transylvania 1919/1970

Imola and the company.

IMOLA   My grandfather returned to Transylvania after the war with a bullet in his leg. He refused to have it removed. And he refused to talk about what happened at the battle of Doberdo. He died 12 years later with the bullet and his story still inside him.

(sings) Kimegyek a doberdói harctérre,

feltekintek a csillagos nagy égre.

Csillagos ég, merre van a magyar hazám,

merre sirat engem az édesanyám?

This is a song the Hungarians soldiers made up about the battle my grandfather fought in. But when I was a was teenager I just thought it was a wonderful, happy dance – csardas!

The company led by Imola do the Csardas dance with music accompaniment.

Beat, the actors sing the first two lines of Happy Birthday slowly, leading into the next scene.

PART 2

Mostly around the time of the Second World War.

18. BIRTHDAY GIRL. London 2014/ Warsaw 1939

Ruth, her mother, and father and the company.

The actors sing the last two lines of happy birthday, now at a normal tempo. Ruth is centre stage holding a wrapped present and smiling at her friends.

RUTH *(laughing)* Thank you so much, but I'm too old for birthdays.

She makes a small turn on herself, as the singing shifts to the Polish Happy Birthday song and Ruth is transported back in time to her 9th Birthday in Poland.

The friends melt away, apart from two, who become her parents hovering at a distance, singing Happy Birthday in Polish, as she starts to open her present. Ruth transforms into herself as a 9 year old child.

The child Ruth unties the ribbons and removes the wrapping paper. She takes out an embroidered bolero and a headdress with ribbons and flowers.

On screen comes a photo Ruth as a child dressed in this bolero and head- dress.

FATHER   Happy Birthday Rutka.

RUTH   It's just what I wanted!

FATHER   Now you can be a proper little Polish girl, huh Mama?

RUTH *(mimes putting on the head dress or bolero)* And I can dance the *krakowiak* and the *mazurka*!

(Sings opening line) Chervone jabluszko pzekrojone na kshyz...

Ruth and her parents remain on stage, continuing the birthday scene silently, as lights up on Annie and dim on previous scene.

19. BIRTHDAY GIRL. Rajkot, India 1939

Annie, Ruth, Ruth's father.

ANNIE *(calling out)* Mummy, Daddy, come and look! It's my best birthday present ever!

(We hear the sound of a pony whinnying.) The Maharajah of Jaipur has lent her to me 'til I'm grown up, because Daddy did him a big favour, you see. She's a little polo pony and she's called Juliana and I'm going to ride her every single day. And my new books have just arrived! A brown paper parcel comes every week with books for us, but sometimes we drive into the bazaar, to the book-store and I can choose. But Daddy says we mustn't go there now because a famous man called Gandhi has come to Rajkot and there are crowds of angry *badmashes* shouting and Daddy says he's dangerous. *(Annie now stands with her arms out while the dherzi (tailor) fits her dress.)* Oh dherz, i-it's so hot standing here with these pins sticking into me and I think I'm going to faint. I hate frocks anyway. I like wearing shorts. But there'll be an elephant at my party and a snake charmer, so I suppose it's worth it. *(counting on her fingers)* Ek, do, teen, char, panch, chay... *(gives up)* well I CAN count

in Hindi – anyway we have lots of servants to look after us, and Mummy says thank goodness or she'd never manage because she's so busy at the club and being head of Girl Guides and organising gramophone concerts and things.

So, there's our bearer who's in charge of everything, and next there's the *kitmagar*, and then the *kansama* who cooks our *tiffin*, and the two *malis* who are our gardeners. Then there's the *bhisti-wallah* – he carries our water in cans on a yoke across his shoulders – and the *dhobi wallah* who takes away our clothes in a big bundle and brings them back all clean and ironed. And the *chokidar*, he's our guard in the daytime, and we have a night-watch man too who creeps around the compound with a torch and a big stick. Then there's the sweeper, he cleans our latrines – and the poor old *punkha wallah* who sits at the end of a long rope tied to a rattan fan on the ceiling and just pulls it for hours and hours. Oh and my *syse*, who looks after the stables. And then there's my *ayah*, who looks after me. I love my ayah NO, ayah – isa mutt karao! No castor oil today, ayah, it's my birthday!

RUTH *(looking round, in awe, whispering)* Marisya, my best friend, has brought me here. It's my first time in a Catholic church, well I've only been to synagogue once – we've never really been religious, because Father's a Marxist, Mother says. I can hear singing, it sounds like angels, the smell of incense fills my nostrils. There are candles everywhere. *(turns to Papa)* Papa! Now I know what I want to be!

FATHER   What's that darling?

RUTH   I want to be a Catholic!

FATHER   You can be whatever you want to be darling, but your choice must be made from knowledge, so before you make up your mind about anything, you must learn!

Ruth squeezes her father's hand by way of thanks and she and father exit.

Lights up on Annie as screen projection comes up of her father in uniform wearing his paghri (turban).

ANNIE   Why can't I be Indian, Daddy? I was born here in India, doesn't that mean I'm Indian? You wear a *paghri* with your uniform, that's Indian isn't it?

Lights fade on Annie and fade up on the next scene to the sound of four sharp knocking sounds, at the fourth knock lights are fully up.

20. THE KNOCK ON THE DOOR.
Vienna 1939

Humpo (Paul), and his mother.

A bedroom in the Humpoletz apartment. On a chair is an opened suitcase packed to the brim. Humpo's mother hands him some Lindt chocolate and some new artist's notebooks. Humpo smiles, touched, and packs them.

MOTHER   Couldn't you just...

HUMPO   What?

MOTHER   Give up your political work, resign from the newspaper – and stay here.

HUMPO   Mutti, please don't be naïve. D'you imagine they'll think – "At last Paul Humpoletz has given up targeting the Nazis with his cartoons, so now we can take him off the list!" No, once on the Führer's hit list, always on the Führer's hit list.

MOTHER I suppose you're right mein Kind. And Prague is a beautiful city. (*She starts to re-fold some of his garments. And as she does so she comes across some of his cartoons tucked beneath his clothes.*) I haven't seen this one. (*We see one of Humpo's gruesome anti-Nazi cartoons on the screen. She leafs through a few more, which flash up briefly on the screen*) I sometimes wish you hadn't been so talented.

HUMPO Thank you Mutti.

MOTHER And look where it got you. And your socialism.

Loud knocks, a sequence of four.

They freeze. Humpo goes to the window and takes a cautious sidelong look at the street outside, then gives a grave nod to his mother, who looks aghast. The knocking picks up again, five knocks, with the loudest knock at the end. Humpo picks up his coat and his suitcase and makes for the window to exit. His mother adjusts her hair, straightens her dress and walks imperiously to the door under music. She turns to face audience as the music is playing, becoming the young Ruth. The lighting shifts as she turns.

21. RE-LOCATION. Warsaw/Simla 1940

Ruth, Narrators.

NARRATOR 1 Ruth was only ten when war broke out. Her whole world was turned upside down.

RUTH   I remember running to my window at the sound of heavy boots marching through the streets. I remember seeing an old man being pulled across the road by his beard. I remember the man in the black shirt coming to our house and saying we have twenty minutes to pack and leave. "Zwanzig Minuten und raus." I remember my mother's look as she replied: "And is your heart as black as your shirt?" I remember his answer, the heavy slap of his hand against her cheekbone. *(Ruth makes a slapping sound with her hands)*

The company become a crowd marching to the Ghetto, under:

RUTH   We and our Jewish neighbours are now marched to the other side of Warsaw. Goodbye childhood, goodbye home, we are now in a crowded room with other strangers in the Ghetto. This is the beginning of the nightmare!

Lights up on Annie, Ruth's neighbours scatter as if they are now busy Indian servants, as the actors make their way to their seats under Annie's speech.

ANNIE   Today we're going on an adventure. All our things and our bedding have been loaded into a cabin carriage on the train because we're going to spend the hot weather up in Simla. Bearer and ayah are coming too but they aren't allowed to sit with us in our compartment, which I think is jolly mean and Mummy thinks so too but she says the stationmaster won't allow it. The train journey will take a whole two days. The only sad thing is I have to leave my pony – and of course that Daddy will come later because he has to stay and do his work.

Train whistle.

NARRATOR 1 One day, looking out of the window, Ruth sees her friend.

RUTH   Marysia!

NARRATOR 2 She's standing on the opposite side of the street from the Ghetto, the side of freedom.

RUTH   I can't call out.

NARRATOR 1 She waves.

RUTH   She shouts something. At first I cannot hear, but then her words hit me like pellets. "Why are you here? Why? Why?" The 'why' reverberates. Why am I here? Why is this all happening. What have I done? The whole world should scream out why? WHY? But there are no answers because there are no words!

Lights down and simultaneously up on the next scene as we hear the three knocks.

22. RE-LOCATION. London 1940

Humpo, Morrie the greengrocer, Policeman.

Humpo's lodgings in London. Three knocks on the door. Humpo, gives a start, uneasy, then opens the door to Morrie, who is standing with a box of vegetables. The scene takes place at the door.

MORRIE   Ah, Mr Hafferlitz.

HUMPO   Humpoletz.

MORRIE   I brought yer the veg you was wanting.

HUMPO   What?

MORRIE *(shouting as to a foreigner)* I brought yer – a selection – of vegetables what you wanted. *(lifting up each item, loud)* Carrot. Onion... *(about to lift up the potato)*

HUMPO   Potato.

MORRIE   Very good! Also, the mustard and cress.

HUMPO   Mustard? No, no I don't eat mustard.

MORRIE   No, no it's a vegetable.

HUMPO   Mustard is a vegetable?

HUMPO *(sighs as he gives up trying to explain)* It's nice in a sandwich. *(mimes making a sandwich)* Bit of marge with it, lovely.

HUMPO   Was ist marge?

MORRIE   Margarine. Like butter. *(said with glottal stop)*

HUMPO   Butter? *(said with glottal stop)* Ah butter.

MORRIE   No butter now though, with the war on. Now – *(makes spreading gesture)* margarine.

HUMPO   I need coupon for this?

MORRIE   Exactly, very good! But if you're nice to Mrs Abrams, round the corner she'll give it you without a coupon, *(gestures)* from underneath the counter.

Paul looks bewildered.

MORRIE   Listen, you have a try of the cress. Maybe you'll enjoy it. That'll be one and ninepence.

Humpo gets a purse out and pays him.

MORRIE   Two bob, threepence change.

A policeman arrives.

POLICEMAN   Which of you gents is *(consulting the paper in his hand)* Mr Humpo...? *(pronounced as in 'BUMP')*

HUMPO   Humpoletz, that's me.

POLICEMAN   I've been instructed to take you with me to the police station sir, under the enemy aliens act. Internment. *(reads the paper)* Looks like they're shipping you off to the Isle of Man.

MORRIE   'Ere, that can't be right. Look, he's just escaped 'itler. So he's hardly the enemy, is 'e?

POLICEMAN   I just have my orders. I'm sure they won't keep you there for long sir, just precautions. I'll wait here while you pack some of your things.

HUMPO   You are saying – I have to go now?

POLICEMAN   If you wouldn't mind sir.

MORRIE   As if you hadn't had enough tzoros.

Humpo doesn't understand.

MORRIE   Yiddish.

HUMPO   I don't speak Yiddish, I'm sorry.

MORRIE   Oh, I was forgetting – German Jews is too high falutin' to speak Yiddish.

HUMPO *(handing the vegetables back to Morrie)* I think I can't use these now.

MORRIE   No, keep them, you might need them. And here, take this back. *(holds out the money)*

HUMPO   Why?

MORRIE   I'm a Jew. Like you. It's with my sympathies. I know what's been going on in Germany.

HUMPO   I'm from Austria…

Morrie shrugs.

HUMPO   … And I'm not a Jew.

Morrie looks at the money in his hand and then back at Humpo.

Light slow fade and sharp up on the next scene.

23. GOODBYE PARENTS. Warsaw 1943

Narrator, Ruth, her father, her mother, her aunt, female guard, male guards, slave factory workers.

NARRATOR Ruth is nearly 13 now.

RUTH   … and my father has managed somehow to get permits for me and my aunt, to work in a leather factory outside Warsaw, and from there to escape with false papers

NARRATOR When it comes to saying good bye to her parents, her mother cannot speak.

FATHER   It's all for the best.

Music under:

Ruth tries not to leave as her aunt leads her away.

RUTH   I don't want to go. *(starts to cry)*

Ruth sees her mother, turned away, shaking with tears. Ruth looks towards her father.

FATHER   Its all for the best, Ruth.

Music over:

Her aunt turns Ruth away from her parents, and as they dissolve away, we hear her father's disembodied voice "Its all for the best, for the best, for the best, for the best…"

RUTH   At the factory, where we are no more than slave labourers, we sleep on the floor, under thin blankets, the women on one side, the men on the other. We are always cold and very hungry. At night we talk in whispers, and nearly always about food. Occasionally I manage to sneak downstairs to the boiler room to meet Pavel. He's a bit older than me, about fifteen and so good looking. We talk, we kiss, we dream.

Work begins at 5.30 in the morning.

We see Ruth and her aunt at work in the factory, along with all the other slave factory workers. A female guard walks by inspecting them. She notices that Ruth is slow in her work.

FEMALE GUARD   What's this, you're taking a nice little holiday now?

AUNT   She's sorry she has some pain from her appendix operation…

FEMALE GUARD   So, where is the pain, exactly?

AUNT   Around here… *(Ruth's aunt pats her own stomach)*

The female guard bends down to touch Ruth's stomach as though sympathetic, then delivers a massive punch to her stomach. Ruth mimes a Munch-like scream and holds her stomach.

FEMALE GUARD   Is that the right place?

RUTH *(trying to hide the pain, faint)* Yes.

FEMALE GUARD   Sure?

RUTH *(a bit louder)* Yes.

FEMALE GUARD So now it will get better! And remember no more little holiday trips. *(exits)*

The slave factory workers return to their work.

ANDREW   Each week the factory workers are marched back into Warsaw, accompanied by armed guards with their dogs, and taken to the Ghetto bathhouse to be de-loused.

We see two guards walking to and fro with their guns.

RUTH   My aunt has a plan.

AUNT *(grabs Ruth and marches her up to the guard, Ruth holding her stomach and looking ill)* She needs the toilet.

The guard who is lighting a cigarette – signals indifference, while the other takes a break.

RUTH   I go to into the toilet and pretend to be sick. I wait for my aunt to knock on the door when the coast is clear.

Ruth's aunt watches the guard through the window, then turning to her niece, she nods to her as she removes her Jewish Star armband, and drops it down the toilet, Ruth copies her.

AUNT   Now it's just a question of walking out of the Ghetto and crossing the road. *(Aunt takes Ruth's hand)* Let's go.

The guard is behind them as they emerge from the toilet building, stubbing out his cigarette, then removing a handkerchief from his pocket and wiping his forehead, as he moves out of frame. Ruth and her aunt turn in the direction of a strong beam of light.

AUNT *(to Ruth who is looking round)* Look straight ahead. Don't run. Look natural...

RUTH *(as they freeze Ruth speaks within the beam of light)* On one side is certain death, the other, probable death. We cross to the other side – from darkness into light.

The impression we get, as the two women are frozen in that beam of light, is of the longest journey ever made. Finally the two women unfreeze, and we understand that they have made it safely to the other side. As they make their gestures of relief towards each other, we hear Ruth's father's disembodied voice: "It's all for the best... for the best... the best... the best... " then the voice is abruptly cut off, as is the beam of light.

We see Ruth standing still, starkly lit, making the sign of the cross.

RUTH   I am now a Catholic. My name is Irena Slawoska.

The light now changes, as Ruth turns and crosses with Annie as she exits.

24. GOODBYE PARENTS. Himalayas, India 1943

Annie, Andrew.

ANNIE   Because of this horrid war, lots of us children have been sent away, so now I'm at boarding school in Naini Tal, which is a hill station in the Himalayas. We can see all the huge mountains with snow on them. The school is called The Hallet War School and our headmaster is a clergyman and we call him Chief and he has enormous ears. I think Mummy's a bit is sad that I've gone and so am I. But it's good fun here, and the best thing is there are boys as well as girls. Mummy and Daddy were furious with our teacher because she wrote in my report 'We do not advise sending Ann to a co-educational school in the future' – and Daddy said she was a thin-lipped bitch.

Lots of us children have fathers in the Indian army and I want this war to stop because it's horrid for Daddy being away fighting in Burma away and it's dangerous. Sometimes I get letters from him, and from Mummy and I keep them in my special Tibetan treasure box, with the photo of them getting married (*this comes up on screen*) and my favourite photo of my pony, and one of Daddy in his uniform.

She takes the last photo from her pocket and kisses it, then shows it to Andrew who is hovering nearby, a military cap tucked under his arm.

ANNIE   My father, in his uniform.

ANDREW (*showing her a photo*) And this is my father in mufti.

A photo of Jack Hawkins comes up on the screen.

ANNIE   He's handsome! Like a film star!

Lights snap down on Annie as the Jack Hawkins photo snaps off the screen.

25. GOODBYE BOMBAY? Bombay 1945

Jack Hawkins (Andrew), Doreen, Major, Brigadier, Colonel Walker.

Andrew is looking at a couple of photos, which come up on the screen under the following speech – one of his father and one of his mother.

ANDREW I don't exist yet, but my future mother, *(turns to the screen as though summoning up the photos of his parents)* actress Doreen Lawrence, and father, actor Jack Hawkins, have just arrived at a military airfield outside Bombay. My father, in the army for the duration of the war and now a colonel, is running all the entertainments for British troops in India and South East Asia. My mother is the leading actress in ENSA's India Repertory Company. They are in love, though actually married to other people, from whom they are both trying, for different reasons, to get divorced. It is shortly after 4.30 in the morning.

Andrew puts on the officer's cap that has been tucked under his arm and becomes Jack.

Military airport, Bombay. It's dark save for lights on the runway.

Three men in officer's uniform form a group and confer, occasionally glancing at their watches. Doreen Lawrence is standing sitting in a car at a distance, powdering her nose.

JACK   Won't be a minute, darling. I'll just go and find out what's going on with the flights.

DOREEN Marvellous.

Jack approaches the officers. Doreen turns the ring on her finger, then takes a script out of her bag and begins to go through her lines.

MAJOR   Didn't see you at the send-off for the Gurkha Rifles last night Colonel.

JACK   No, I was busy.

The Major spots Doreen in the car.

MAJOR   I say, isn't that the dishy Doreen Lawrence you've got in your car?

JACK   Yes, I'm trying to get her on a flight to Calcutta. Do you know what might be going that way this morning?

MAJOR   Room for two is it, Jack? *(checking his watch)* Four forty-five. There was supposed to be one going at 0500 hrs, but...

JACK   Actually, Major, I do need space for two, because there's her bearer. I need to get to Singapore.

COLONEL You'll be lucky!

JACK   I really have to get there by tonight. I mean it would be a shame if I didn't, as I've got Noel Coward and Gracie Fields arriving tomorrow. They've got nowhere to stay and the theatre they're due to perform in is a complete wreck.

A Brigadier arrives.

BRIGADIER Ah, Hawkins, you're here. Look, there's a delay on all air traffic this morning. Not clear why. Orders from HQ. Some major op. apparently. We should have more news shortly. Is that your car,

Hawkins? Can you tell your driver to turn his bloody headlights off?

JACK   Brigadier.

Jack returns to the car. The colonel goes upstage to find out more news.

JACK   Kill the headlights, Corporal.

DOREEN   Well? Any joy?

JACK   No sign of anything yet.

DOREEN   Are we going to be able to get on a plane?

JACK   There are planes, but nothing's moving. There's some kind of delay. *(takes Doreen's hand)* If only we could both stay here, together. *(spots the colonel returning to the officers and speaking intently to them)* Ah, looks like Major's got some news. I'll just go and find out.

Jack goes upstage, intercepts Colonel Walker on his return to the huddle of officers. Doreen practices her lines, working on her American accent.

DOREEN   "Oh really, Captain, that'd be way beyond the call of duty – and anyhow I've already agreed to spend the week in New Jersey–" *(tries this a few times)*

Jack returns to the car, seemingly a bit knocked off balance. Meanwhile Walker rejoins the other officers and we see him relaying the news.

DOREEN   Did you find anything out?

JACK   There aren't going to be any flights today, I'm afraid.

DOREEN   What none at all?

JACK   No, everything's grounded.

DOREEN   What about Singapore? Who's going to take care of Noel and Gracie?

JACK   Seems like something rather more important's come up, darling.

Music to indicate end of 2nd Section.

PART 3

Mostly though not entirely in 1950s

26. RABBITS. Tokyo 1952

Togo, Narrator.

The scene title comes up as Togo is looking at family photos. He pauses at each one of the photos, which then comes up on the screen. Softly he names each family member, seemingly as an act of memory and a return to his childhood in Japan.

TOGO　　母

[Haha]

NARRATOR　Mother.

TOGO　　父。

[Chichi]

NARRATOR　Father.

TOGO　　上の姉。

[Ueno ané Yoko]

NARRATOR　Senior elder sister, Yoko.

TOGO　　下の兄。

[Shitano ani]

NARRATOR　Junior elder brother.

TOGO　　末っ子の私。たぶん6歳。

[Suekkono watashi, tabun roku sai]

NARRATOR Youngest child, me, aged six maybe.

TOGO   下の姉、素子。

[Shitano ané]

NARRATOR Junior elder sister, Motoko.

TOGO (*lying down*) 素子、夜、布団で寝てるとき、 覚えてるかな？

[Motoko, yoru futonde neterutoki, oboeteirukana?]

NARRATOR Motoko, remember how at night we would lie on the futon?

TOGO   天井に映る影を見てたよね。

[Tenjô-ni utsuru kage-o miteitayo-ne.]

NARRATOR And look up at the shadows on the ceiling and see...

TOGO   ウサギ！

[Usagi!]

NARRATOR Rabbits!

We hear the sound of the two children laughing.

TOGO (*in English*) Sweet Motoko. You tried to protect me with your laughter. But the walls were paper thin and I could hear our parents' arguing, and my mother begging my father not to shout so loud or we would hear. They were arguing about my eldest brother who became a member of the Japanese Communist Party after the war. (*looks up at the ceiling*) The rabbits have gone.

27. SOAP-BOX EVE. Colindale 1956

Narrator, Harry Pollit, Eve Cohen (Norma).

NARRATOR Harry Pollit, long term General Secretary of the British Communist Party, now aged 66, and a sick man, is sitting in his living room.

Eve when she speaks has a Liverpool accent.

HARRY *(indicating a small wooden box or crate, Northern accent)* Right try that for size. You're gonna have to get a bigger soapbox than that if anyone's gonna clap eyes on yer. Now face them lads and make sure yer look some of them in the eye, get their attention before you even start. Go-on show me.

Eve makes a show of sharply scrutinising an imaginary audience of workers.

Right then off you go lass.

EVE *(straight out, as though to imaginary workers, stiff)* Ladies and Gentlemen. Workers. Fellow workers. Comrades. 'Comrades', won't go down too well d'ya think, Harry, after Hungary? *(stepping down from the soap box)*

HARRY Hungary be buggered. I have no problem with our Russian comrades going into Hungary to deal with them counter-revolutionary fascists, even though I do have a problem with Premier Krushchev and his cowardly denunciation of Comrade Stalin. *(looks at the framed photo of Stalin on his wall)* I miss him lass, I do.

EVE And you've actually met him, Harry.

HARRY Oh ay, many's the time.

EVE   Amazing! To think I've had tea with a man who's had tea with Comrade Stalin!

HARRY   It weren't tea lass, I can tellya. He were a great leader. A great socialist. And no-one can take that away from him.

EVE   It's all lies then, isn't it Harry? Some of our best friends have left the party since those/ revelations.

HARRY *(cutting in before she can finish)* Sometimes sacrifices have to be made for the greater good Eve. You know that.

Harry is silent.

EVE   Look Harry, I've got my entire Jewish family on my back with all this new stuff that's come out about Stalin and his so-called anti-Jewish purges. But if you think it's all just propaganda which I think it is...

HARRY   All I can say to you Eve love, is that *(pointing at Stalin's photo)* he's staying up there as long as I'm alive.

Beat, while Eve tries and fails to 'read' his answer, then:

HARRY   So up on that soap box lass. Call 'em comrades if yer like, but I'd just call 'em "lads", plain and simple.

EVE   Lads? Isn't that cheeky coming from me?

HARRY   I was your age when I spoke at the docks and 'lads' did the job then.

EVE   You changed history that day.

HARRY   Aye, I won't deny it were a right good victory when those dockers refused to board a ship carrying munitions aimed at toppling the new Soviet Republic.

Eighteen months of campaigning and strikes and we got the government to pull back.

(miming Churchill) Under these pressures Mr Lloyd George has been constrained to advise the Polish government that the British Government cannot take any action against the new Soviet Government.

Now he were a good speaker whatever you think of his politics. So remember – gestures, moderating your voice, familiar but firm, and above all...

EVE   Content. No blathering. *(getting up her soap box, to audience)* Lads, I've come to speak to you today...

Fade down and focussed lighting on Togo as he strides into the space of the next scene shouting in Japanese.

28. DISGRACE. Tokyo/London 1950s

Togo's father (Togo), Narrator, Paul's father (Paul).

Togo as his father, puts on his kimono, tightens his obi, then strides into the middle of the stage shouting in Japanese:

IGAWA-SAN どこにいるんだ！隠れてるのか？

[Dokoni irunda! Kakureterunoka?] *(Where is that boy! Where is the thief hiding?)*

NARRATOR You seem very angry Mr Igawa.

IGAWA-SAN My son makes me angry. He stole a travel pass. From the stationery shop.

ここに連れてきなさい！

[Kokoni tsurete kinasai!] *(Bring him here!)*

NARRATOR Why did he want to steal a travel pass?

IGAWA-SAN It does not matter why. It matters that he steals.

HUMPO My son also steals.

IGAWA-SAN So desu-ka? What do you do about it?

HUMPO Sometimes I hit him.

IGAWA-SAN Yes?

HUMPO Yes. Sometimes with my hand, sometimes with a stick. I don't know what else to do.

IGAWA-SAN I don't hit my son.

HUMPO Well perhaps you don't need to hit your son. What are you going to do to him?

IGAWA-SAN I must take him to the police box.

HUMPO I did zis.

IGAWA-SAN To apologise to the police.

HUMPO How old is your son?

IGAWA-SAN He is seven. How old is your son?

HUMPO My son is ten. How often does your son steal?

IGAWA-SAN This is the first time.

HUMPO Mine steals all the time, he steals from everywhere and from everyone. He lies and he steals and he is not fit to be my son.

Igawa-san nods in agreement.

HUMPO I was a captain in the Austro-Hungarian army in the first world war. I was captured by the Russians and spent four years as a prisoner in Siberia. I escaped and I made my way to Moscow, that's nearly 4, ooo miles. And this boy does nothing. He only brings disgrace on my name.

IGAWA-SAN Disgrace. Exactly. I was a member of the Japanese parliament in the last war. After the war I was barred from public office for five years, and I've only just been able to stand for parliament again and been re-elected. And now my youngest son is a thief and my eldest son disgraces me, making communist speeches to crowds at the railway station. He is banned from the house.

HUMPO This is what I plan to do also with my son.

IGAWA-SAN But your son is ten. How can you ban him?

HUMPO I am sending him away?

IGAWA-SAN Where?

HUMPO To Switzerland. To live with a Swiss family in the mountains. He will learn from them. He will learn to be a cow-herd. *(sound of cow bell)*

Lights fade down.

29. LOVE AND WAR. Transylvania 1950s

Imola, Matild (Imola), Janos.

The scene title comes up in the style of a silent movie caption This silent movie caption style continues during the scene. Piano music in the style of traditional silent movie accompaniment underscores the captions.

IMOLA *(to audience, in Hungarian and then in English)*

Ez egy tortenet a szerelemrol es a haborurol. A nagynenem mindig olyan szomorunak tunt. Egy nap edesanyam elmeselte miert volt Matild mindig szomoru.

This is a story about love and war. A story about my aunt, my mother's sister Matild. My aunt always seemed so sad and one day my mother told me why.

A series of captions appear on screen, while we watch Matild and Janos on stage.

[CAPTION] Once upon a time in a far away place called Transylvania the land of forests and wolves, two young people fell in love, Matild and a young man called Janos.

[CAPTION] But her family refused to allow her to marry him because they were rich and he was very poor.

[CAPTION] Then came the second world war and Janos was called away to fight. Before he left, they had one last meeting in secret.

We see a ghostly faded photo of them up on the screen.

[CAPTION] " I'm coming back Tilda. I promise"

[CAPTION] "I will wait for you Janos"

[CAPTION] Years passed. The war ended But Janos did not return and Matild's parents forced her to marry a rich man from the next village.

[CAPTION] Then one day many years later, Janos returned, finally released from a prison camp in Russia.

[CAPTION] Once again they met in secret, but she was now a mother of two children...

[CAPTION] and he was a man with half a face.

Imola steps into the scene as her aunt Matild, carrying a small baby wrapped in a bundle. Togo joins her as Janos. They face each other, in profile to the audience, with the uninjured side of Janos's face to the audience.

Seconds pass as they take each other in, she with another man's child in her arms, he with a half-destroyed face.

[CAPTION] "I kept my promise Tilda."

[CAPTION] "They made me marry him."

[CAPTION] Do you still love me? Can you still love me now that I look like this?"

Janos embraces her, taking in the baby in his embrace.

[CAPTION] "How can you ask?"

[CAPTION] "Then come away with me, with the children. I will love them as my own."

Long pause, then Matild pulls away from the embrace.

[CAPTION] I can't Janos, I can't.

MUSIC.

Imola now steps forward as herself.

IMOLA *(in Hungarian and then in English)*

Evek multan Janos megnosult, felesegul vett egy lanyt a falubol.Matild szerelem nelkuli hazassagban elt elete vegeig. Janos volt elete nagy szerelme.

In the end Janos married someone else. Mathild stayed in a loveless marriage and Janos remained the love of her life.

Final caption "THE END"

30. SKYPE 2. London/Tokyo 2014/1945

Togo, his wife, his father, his mother, a woman in a kimono.

A continuation of the Skype session from Scene 1.

We can hear Yoko but we cannot see her, just her Skype logo image on the big screen. Togo's wife, wearing her potter's apron, is sitting next to him.

TOGO   Yes, the children are fine, Yoko. They're coming to us for Christmas.

TOGO'S WIFE *(holds up a ceramic sake flask)* I made this for you for new year, and a set of cups, it's my new glaze. I'll post them later.

YOKO   It's beautiful. Dômo arigato.

Beat.

TOGO   So – you got my email with my question?

YOKO   Ee.

TOGO   So you were all in Tokyo when it happened?

Yoko hesitates, then.

YOKO   We were, mother and the children.

TOGO   And father?

YOKO   He was in his constituency.

Silence while Togo tries to take this in.

TOGO *(shocked)* What? Really? Why did no one ever tell me?

Togo's wife reaches out for Togo's hand

YOKO   We hardly ever talked about it. And not in front of you.

Music or sound underscore.

YOKO   Mother took all of us there by train.

TOGO   Mother took you all there!

YOKO   We didn't know then that it was dangerous.

Music or sound underscore, played live on stage.

TOGO   It must have taken a whole day, no more, to get there.

YOKO   I was only ten. I just remember passing through a city that was completely in ruins. But when we finally did get there...

Music or sound underscore.

YOKO   There was no transport to take us to father's place...

Music or sound underscore.

YOKO   ... so we walked and walked and walked.

Music or sound underscore.

YOKO   I saw people carried away on stretchers

Music or sound underscore.

YOKO   And that's when I thought that maybe father was dead.

Sound of water dripping.

YOKO   And all I could think of was how thirsty I was. And suddenly we saw a water pipe with a tap, in the middle of burnt ruins. (*Increased sound of water dripping.*) I rushed up to it and I drank and drank and drank. We all did. We didn't know what we know now.

A series of eery bell-like sounds start to emerge.

YOKO   We were on the outskirts of Nagasaki by now. I remember everything was very dark but we could just see the mountains.

Lights up on Jack and Doreen in their previous location for a continuation of their earlier Scene 26.

The bells carry over into the following scene.

DOREEN   What is it? What's happened?

JACK   It seems that some sort of large bomb has been dropped on Japan.

We now hear crackly, recorded extracts of President Harry Truman's atomic bomb television announcement in August 1945 intercut and slightly under the following:

TRUMAN   It is an atomic bomb...

JACK   News has just come through. A new weapon, apparently.

TRUMAN   ... It is a harnessing of the of basic power of the universe...

YOKO   And then we saw father.

TRUMAN   ... the force from which the sun draws its power has been loosed...

DOREEN   So, that could mean the end of the war?

JACK   It could indeed.

Lights fade down on Jack and Doreen, but they remain visible. Lights fade up on the Nagasaki scene.

TRUMAN What has been done, is the greatest achievement in organised history.

A bell sounds. The pace of the Skype 2 scene now slows down as though being remembered in slow motion

Bell sounds. We see Togo as his father, in kimono.

YOKO   We saw father. Coming out of a small wooden house, its shutters all broken.

Bell sounds.

YOKO   But he wasn't alone.

Bell sounds. We see a woman in kimono, emerging after him. She stares nervously at Togo's mother.

Bell sounds.

We see Togo's mother approaching. The woman moves to stand behind Togo's father. There is a pause, then the woman bows to Togo's mother, who hesitates fractionally before returning her bow.

Bell sounds.

Togo's father steps forward towards his wife. She moves right up to him and fixes him with a stare. We feel the tension. Then, slowly, she bends her head and lets it rest on his shoulder. He is alive!

Throughout Yoko's narration, Togo's English wife has remained seated, totally engrossed in the story.

At the end of the scene we become aware of the other couple on stage Doreen and Jack standing together Doreen's head now on Jack's shoulder.

Togo moves back to his place at the computer and connects with his wife.

Music to indicate end of section.

INTERVAL

PART 4

Revolutionary times: the 1960s, 70s, and 80s

31. IF YOU REMEMBER IT, YOU WEREN'T THERE. 1960s

The company.

ANNIE *(mike in hand, reading out the scene title)* "If you remember it, you weren't there." Too right.

John takes the mike. Spotlight on John.

JOHN   Well I was at Woodstock...

NORMA   Wow!

JOHN   ... and I don't remember much. I do remember the journey out there – me and my friends just thought we were going to hear some bands, not realising the magnitude of the event, and on the way we got stuck on this little country road from about midnight till four or five in the morning. It was amazing, it was the best traffic jam ever! *(laughter)* People sitting on trunks of cars, passing bottles of wine, beer, marijuana. And after it was all over and we got back to New York city we realised that that weekend we'd created the third-largest city in New York state! There were like half a million people there. But on the other hand, because I was em *(drops voice)* inebriated on various substances, *(laughter)* all I can really remember is Jimmy Hendrix closing it with... and not much else.

TREVOR *(taking the mike)* I never had a cigarette till I was 21 and never tasted alcohol till I was 25. The

60s for me was all about the folk scene. I was into Pentangle and that sort of thing *(sings)* 'All around my hat I will wear the green willow...'

As Trevor sings, some of the actors may join in. Jasmina takes the mike as Trevor stands down, continuing to sing softly under:

JASMINA I lived in the heart of Chelsea in the swinging 60s, one house away from Margaret Thatcher, not that that meant anything then, just off the Kings Road, and I'm afraid it all more or less passed me by. I was too serious as a drama student. I went to one pop concert which was the Beatles in Finsbury Park...

NORMA I went to that one!

ANDREW I was there.

ANNIE Me too.

JASMINA ... And a girl bit my hand because she was having an orgasm and I didn't know what an orgasm was at the time, she was screaming and gasping and groaning. She was only about 12 she probably didn't realise what was happening to her.

TOGO Of course we had the Beatles but for me, the 60s was a political time. Like in France in '68. There were a lot of demonstrations against the renewal of the US-Japan Security Treaty. The riot police looked like Darth Vader with their great big shields and lethal spiked boots, terrifying! Hundreds of them started charging at us when the commander shouted いて まえ！[Ite mae!], which means something like "Kill them!"

NORMA I remember being at the Edinburgh Festival, and being locked in a room with the People Show and this bloke, Jeff Nuttall, went round cutting people's ties off and smearing jam over their faces, and everybody allowed it!

PAUL   I was a bouncer at the Marquee club, Manfred Mann, the Animals. I was a pathetic bouncer – I'd very, very courageously walk up to people knocking a couple of coke bottles together and ask them to desist – 'Ere that's enough of that!

NORMA   I remember going to this big party in Hampstead and there was no food, just this enormous cake. And I remember stuffing myself with it. I was starving! And then being in this huge yawning garden with all these faces looking at me and just sitting there absolutely terrified, too naïve to realise what was in that cake!

ANNIE   It was a sort of mad period. It felt as though you could do almost anything you liked. Not much money but an endless amount of treats. I fell in with a crowd of Canadian hippy bikers with names like Roach and Twitch and Crash and Smot – one of them always crashed on our floor. I had my own bike too for a while, a Triumph Tiger Cub which eventually got stolen before it could do too much damage. So I led these two parallel lives: one as a working actor, and one with these stoned hippies.

IMOLA   Drugs? In Romania? No. Shake, Twist, Beatles, the Rolling Stones – it wasn't allowed. We loved Hair but it was banned. But we were too nervous to play these records at parties. I was crazy about Hair, the music.

From now on the actors start to cut into each other's speeches, sometimes overlapping. The whole things start to become a psychedelic experience, underscored by the psychedelic lighting.

ANDREW The first time I took LSD I was 18, with a couple of friends in the mountains of Snowdonia.

ANNIE   I can remember my first trip. It was in Canada with crazy Tom…

ANDREW And at first nothing happened. And then, it must have been about half an hour after we'd taken the tabs and I was laughing hysterically because my friend Mike had turned into a monkey.

RUTH   All I remember is all of a sudden the space opened up and I became very small in this gigantic space and was very, very frightened…

ANNIE   … What I remember were the colours. I've never, ever experienced such intensity of colour – of seeing the redness of tomatoes, the greenness of cucumber…

ANDREW … And for one split second I had a sort of insight that I had totally gone, I was somewhere else altogether…

RUTH   … and then when I looked at the young guy who gave me the LSD, it was terrifying I saw his face changing, becoming old and decrepit and disfigured like an ogre…

ANDREW When we got back to my friend's house, I felt like the floor had dropped out of everything really…

RUTH   … and it was the most frightening experience of my life.

ANDREW … and the last lines of 'Kubla Khan' were going around in my head…

RUTH   ... which was just as well because who knows what would have happened if it had been a wonderful experience!

ANDREW ... "Beware, beware! Weave a circle round him thrice. And close your eyes with holy dread/For he on honeydew hath fed and drunk the milk of paradise"

RUTH   I mean we were looking for deeper meaning, searching for some sort of inner truth.

Trevor and company sing part of the Aquarius song from Hair.

When the moon is in the seventh house

And Jupiter aligns with Mars

Then peace will guide the planets

And love will steer the stars

This is the dawning of the age of Aquarius
The age of Aquarius, Aquarius, Aquarius Aquarius, Aquarius

Let the sunshine Let the sunshine in

The sunshine in...

The singing is interrupted by a burst of motorbike sound leading into the next scene. Transition music e.g. Volare or La Bamba

32. WHERE IS ANNA LAGANÀ?
Italy 1969

Andrew, Stefano, Stefano's mother (La Signora), the cook, and the company.

Motorbike sound. Lights up on Andrew, perched behind Stefano on a motorbike.

ANDREW *(nervously hanging on to Stefano)* So I'm 18. I'm staying with an Italian family to teach English to their son who's about my age. He's got this rather tasty Ducati motorbike and we tear around Rome on it.

Andrew and Stefano suddenly both veer to one side as the bike takes a corner.

STEFANO *(shouts)* You iz okay Andrew?

ANDREW *(shouting back)* "Are OK" Stefano. "You are OK".

STEFANO *(taking this as a question, loud)* Si, I'ma okaya, no problem.

The bike now swerves in the opposite direction as Stefano spies a friend and waves, shouting "Ciao Giulia", to Andrew's disconcertion, under:

ANDREW It was obvious from the start on that Stefano wasn't particularly interested in learning English. The PR woman for Columbia Pictures in Rome found this Italian family for me as a favour to my parents. The father was some sort of concrete magnate. But by the time I got there...

The bike screeches to a halt as they arrive at Stefano's house.

... he had dumped his wife for a younger woman, and what remained of the family had moved into a smart apartment in Parioli, a leafy and salubrious suburb in Rome. *(getting off his bike)* There was just La Signora *(greets la Signora)* Buona sera, Signora...

The Signora acknowledges Andrew with a smile, then her attention focuses on Stefano, abandoned like her, by il Signore.

SIGNORA *(mournful, to her son)* Stefano – ma che fai??

ANDREW … And the cook.

The cook in an apron rushes up to Stefano and plants a kiss on his cheek.

COOK Stefano, vuoi qualcosa da bere?

Stefano jerks away, moody. The two women catch each other's eye as they observe Stefano's moodiness under:

ANDREW I think Stefano was having some sort of oedipal meltdown. His main interest apart from a simmering loathing for his bourgeois parents was to track down the woman with whom he had experienced an explosive sexual epiphany – Anna Laganà. About four weeks after my arrival he suddenly announced:

STEFANO I 'ave to go. Ciao. Bye-bye.

ANDREW Sorry?

STEFANO *(gestures a knife sliding across his throat)* Basta my family! I go. They can fucka.

ANDREW 'Off'. Fuck off.

STEFANO Grazie, yes. Fuckaoffa. Tomorrow I go Sicily.

ANDREW Why Sicily?

I really liked Rome.

STEFANO To see Anna Laganà.

ANDREW And what the hell am I supposed to do? Ma che cosa faccio io?

STEFANO *(with a shrug)* You can come.

ANDREW Good! So we bomb down to her supposed address in Sicily. But it's in a slum, like I've never seen, with an open drain in the middle of the street.

Stefano starts knocking at doors, lighting indicates it's getting dark and creepy. The suspicious slum dwellers opening the doors, some just a crack, some coming out and standing arms-crossed as Stefano continues to pose the question:

STEFANO Scusi, conosce la casa di Anna Laganà? Conosce Anna Laganà? Sa dove sta?

ANDREW And people would just go *(with a shrugging movement)* 'e'.

STEFANO Somebodya follow us, he got a knife. Donta look back.

They run off, then arrive at the café on a motor bike.

ANDREW A few of weeks later we're back with La Signora, and we're all out at a café near their summer residence in Ostia – just down the beach from where I'd stayed as a child when my father was filming Ben Hur. And gradually more and more people seem to fixate on this tiny television perched up on a shelf, except for Stefano who's still obsessing about the elusive Anna Laganà.

Stefano and Andrew are lounging a distance away from everyone else.

STEFANO What to do, eh, Andrew, what to do?

Throughout their exchange we see and hear the patrons of the café including La Signora, and the cook, getting more and more drawn to the tiny TV screen, with Andrew occasionally craning to see what the interest is, but having to pay attention to the love-sick Stefano.

STEFANO She notta in Firenze. She notta in her home in Sicilia...

ANDREW *(his eyes now on the TV)* Well you don't actually know that.

CAFÉ PATRON *(in disbelief)* Non! NON! Sono proprio arrivati sulla luna.

COOK   Non è possibile! Questa non é la luna! La luna è fatta di formagio.

SIGNORA Incredibile! Guardi, guardi, Stefano! Vieni qui Andrea

CAFÉ PATRON *(dreamy)* Incredibile!

We hear a faint crackly from the TV:

TV   Columbia, Columbia this is Houston.

SIGNORA Vieni qui Stefano, Andrea – guardi, sta scendendo!

TV *(Neil Armstrong's voice)* That's one small step for man, a giant leap for mankind...

COOK   Ma, non è possibile! La luna è fatta di formaggio.

Andrew tries to move away from Stefano towards the TV but his arm is grabbed by Stefano.

STEFANO She, a woman of the people. No like my parents.

TV   ... progressing beautifully they're setting up the flag now...

STEFANO Anna, Anna Laganà: most beautiful, appassionata...

TV They've got the flag up now you can see the stars and stripes.

Overlapping:

CAFÉ PATRON *(cynical)* Ah, bandoliere Americano!

CAFÉ PATRON Silenzio!

CAFÉ PATRON Un miracolo... miracolo!

CAFÉ PATRON Meravigliosa!

COOK Basta!

CAFÉ PATRON Che cosa stupenda!

SIGNORA Si, si, stupenda.

NEIL ARMSTRONG'S VOICE Are you getting the TV picture now, Houston?

TV Neil, yes we are getting the TV pictures.

Under Stefano's next speech. Andrew finally manages to walk away from Stefano towards the crowd around the TV.

STEFANO *(calling out to Andrew)* Hey. I thinka you are my friend, no?

ANDREW And that's how I almost missed it. The most momentous event in human history – well, arguably — sidelined by that other event that always seems to be so momentous to individual lives, l'amore.

Three months later, I'm starting my first term at Oxford reading medieval history. But it just didn't make any sense after my Italian summer, experiencing history in

Rome and Florence. *(to friend)* I'm just not interested in the 12th century anymore.

FRIEND *(posh voice)* Well why don't you change? I'm changing to Sanskrit.

ANDREW Holy shit?!

Andrew swivels to face his disapproving tutor

TUTOR   This is a very grave decision.

ANDREW *(to tutor)* I know, sir. *(to audience)* But I made it. Switched to English literature, inspired by my Italian odyssey, that unforgettable summer of light and heat and motorbikes, and the intense longing of this young Italian guy, not for material ambition or for studying, but for sensuality and for love.

Under this last speech the café crowd transform into workers at the Merseyside docks, wearing cloth caps with Norma as Eve, standing on a chair, gesturing to them, inspired by the tutelage of Harry Pollit.

33. THE BRITISH ROAD TO SOCIALISM. Merseyside Docks 1960s

Eve (Norma), the company, Norma.

Actors begin to move towards Eve, putting on workers' cloth caps as they do so, to become the crowd Eve is addressing with gesticulations.

EVE   And so lads, I'm standing up here in front of you today on behalf of the Labour Party, the trade unions and the whole Labour movement

Freeze for a second or two, then Eve starts to take off her outer clothes to reveal a glorious riot of colour in the clothing underneath as Eve 'transforms' into Norma, while the company move away and then start to form a queue for bread in communist Romania.

NORMA   That was my mother Eve. She was quite a performer. Is that where I get it from? She was a tough act to follow though. Both my parents were. High-minded, idealistic – blinkered. Dedicated to the Communist Party and achieving the British Road to Socialism, with weekly family meetings run on party lines addressing your remarks through the chair – my Dad usually. That was the culture we grew up in, my brothers and I – the trade union movement, marches, campaigns – for better housing, workers' rights, CND, the miners' strikes, the Vietnam war. We lived and breathed it as kids. For my parents, the Soviet Union and Eastern Europe were the utopias – for me it was Liverpool, home of the Beatles and after we moved south as a family – swinging London.

Norma, as her younger self, starts jiving, then does some hand-jiving, then the twist.

34. KOMMUNIZMUS. London/Bucharest 1960s/70s

Imola, her friend Edit, Norma, the company.

Lights up on another part of the stage. Imola as her younger self, is part of the queue, looking with great interest at Norma across a big divide. She is with Edit. They start to copy Norma's dance movements.

IMOLA *(in Hungarian, calling out to Norma across the stage)* Mi ez a tanc?

[What is name of this dance?]

NORMA *(calling back, Liverpool accent)* Ye what?

EDIT *(Hungarian accent)* My friend wants to know the name of that dance?

NORMA   It's called the Twist. *(calling across as they continue to dance the Twist)* What country you's lot from then?

IMOLA AND EDIT Romania.

NORMA   Roma what?

IMOLA   Ro-m-a-ni-a.

NORMA   Oh, you're Romanian.

IMOLA   Hungarian. From Transylvania

EDIT   Which used to belong to Hungary, but now belongs to Romania.

NORMA *(a bit fazed)* Right. Hungary's communist, though isn't it.

EDIT   And so is Romania.

NORMA   Cool! *(proud)* My parents are communists. My Dad says we're on the British road to socialism. But you've gone all the way – to communism

IMOLA *(with disdain)* You like Kommunizmus?

NORMA   Course, it's the ideal society isn't it.

IMOLA *(to Norma)* I show you Kommunismus.

Beckoned by Imola, Norma gingerly crosses the stage.

IMOLA *(to Norma, pointing)* Is queue.

NORMA   Oh we have those.

There's a disturbance and a groaning from the queue which disperses and re-forms as a queue for coffee.

EDIT   ... and sometimes like today – people queue, then all bread finished. (*We see Imola and Edit get to the front of this new queue.*) Queue for coffee always very long.

IMOLA (*yawning, pointing at her watch, then pulls up her collar against the cold, in Hungarian*) Harom ora. [Three o'clock.]

EDIT   3 o'clock. In the morning.

IMOLA (*In Hungarian, to Norma*) Apamert allok sorban. [I'm queuing for my father.]

EDIT   She save all her coffee coupons for her father.

NORMA   It's a bit cold, out here. I'm not really dressed for it. Anyway, I've got to get to my Saturday job. I work in Boots. (*crosses the stage*)

EDIT (*calling after her*) Boots is also big problem and shoes.

NORMA   No no, Boots is a chemist's. You can come if you like.

EDIT   We cannot! We have to leave passports with police. And we must only go to communist country.

NORMA   You're joking.

EDIT   No is true.

NORMA   Oh come on, it's only a play!

Imola and her Edit look at each other, look around, nervous, then Imola turns up her coat collar and they sneak across the stage, hoping not to be spotted.

NORMA   This is it, Boots, in Muswell Hill. It's just a small Boots. Nothing fancy.

The lighting becomes magical. Music under: Imola as she moves round the shop transfixed. She takes a bottle of shampoo from one of the shelves.

IMOLA *(reading the label, full of wonder)* "Shampoo"! *(to Edit)* Sampon?

EDIT *(to Imola)* Igen.

NORMA   What's up with her?

EDIT   We don't see shampoo in our shops for seven years.

NORMA   You're kidding.

IMOLA *(to Norma, grim)* Kommunismus!

Imola continue to wander round the goods on the shelves, marvelling. She reaches for a bar of soap, enraptured.

IMOLA   Szappan!

Imola presses the soap to her nose, ecstatic. Edit sneaks across to join Imola who passes her the soap to smell.

EDIT   Sometimes we don't have soap and her mother make it for her.

Imola's attention is now caught by a row of condoms. She takes down a pack. She reads the label.

IMOLA *(mispronouncing)* "Feather... lite"

EDIT *(correcting her pronunciation)* Featherlite.

IMOLA   What it means?

EDIT *(reads)* "Greater fit and natural sensation"

BOTH *(realisation)* Ovszer! Condoms!

NORMA *(looking around, embarrassed)* Shh.

The queue prick up their ears and in a flash, all turn up their collars and rush across the stage to Boots. They stampede the shop, snatching the condom packets off the shelves and stuffing them in their pockets.

NORMA *(to the queue crowd)* 'ere, whatye doing? *(Ignoring her they rush back to 'Romania'. Calling after)* That's stealing that is!

IMOLA   You don't understand. We have big problem. We don't have in Romania. Is not allowed.

NORMA   Really? So what do you use, the Pill?

EDIT   Nothing! Ceauşescu, our 'big communist leader', he say every woman should have five children. We have big problem if we have – *(lowers her voice)* accident. Terrible for women. Many women die. Abortion not allowed. You can go to prison.

IMOLA *(urgent)* I can take one more?

EDIT   Me too?

NORMA *(suddenly solemn, looking around)* Go on then.

Imola and Edit scurry back to Romania, their pockets full of condoms.

Norma looks at her watch, then hurriedly grabs a banner on a pole and dashes to the front of what become a line of demonstrators in the next scene.

35. THE DRAFT. New York 1972

The company, John, psychiatrist.

An image of an anti-Vietnam war demonstration in London comes up on screen.

The company form a line behind Norma who is holding up a placard saying 'Young Communist League Against the War in Vietnam". Other demonstrators hold placards saying "End the War in Vietnam', and chanting Ho, Ho, Ho Chi Minh. The snaking line files off, leaving John centre stage with a bandanna round his head, and hippy style long hair.

On screen an image of Kent State anti-Vietnam demo.

JOHN   So I'm 20 years old, a student, and my luck, my number just came up in the lottery for the draft. And there's no way I'm gonna go. No way! Anyone I know that's been out there, either he's come back dead or totally fucked up. And anyway I'm against this war. We've all been on demonstrations, sit-ins. So, the night before my first meeting with the Draft Board my buddies came round and we did all kinds of stuff, dope, LSD, booze – and I still passed the physical! So I tell them I have some mental problems and they refer me to this psychiatrist. This morning my girlfriend dresses me to look kinda weird and now I'm shitting myself. I don't know what I'm gonna say exactly or do.

Psychiatrist Doctor Fisher approaches him.

DR FISHER Mr Moriatis?

JOHN   Moraitis.

DR FISHER Would you come this way.

They enter the doctor's office and they both sit down on either side of the doctor's desk. At a certain point in the scene John starts to encroach on the doctor's desk space, playing with objects on it. The more John leans forward and comes into his space, the more the man withdraws from him in his body language, till it reaches some kind of crescendo.

DR FISHER I'm Dr Fisher. I'm a psychiatrist. The draft board has referred you to me to assess your psychological condition. Will you just confirm your date of birth?

JOHN August 5th 1950.

DR FISHER So you're twenty one years old.

JOHN Correct.

DR FISHER And I see you're a student at City University?

JOHN Yes sir.

DR FISHER I understand you told the board you have some sort of psychiatric condition, mental problems.

JOHN It's just, I take LSD sometimes.

DR FISHER Really? How many times have you taken LSD Mr Moraitis?

John's behaviour starts going a bit more blurred around the edges as he occupies more and more of the doctor's desk, and starts playing with objects on the doctor's desk.

JOHN Twenty times? Maybe thirty?

DR FISHER 20 or 30 times! You are aware that lysergic acid diethylamide is a dangerous and prohibited drug that can induce psychosis. What kind of effect has it had on you?

JOHN   Well I have these sort of flashes. Everything's going straight and then I'm walking along and kind of suddenly I see a burst of something, in the sky.

DR FISHER Like what – God or...?

JOHN   No it's like a star is bursting. It'll suddenly flash, and then flash. I'll be walking along and the sidewalk will suddenly jump up at me.

DR FISHER The sidewalk will jump up at you?

JOHN   Yuh I'm just walking along and it will go. *(gesticulates, holding one of the objects on the doctor's desk e.g. a heavy paper weight causing the doctor to back off a bit)* Kinda in waves. And sometimes I'll look at someone's face *(looks deeply into the psychiatrist's face)* and it'll start to move a bit.

DR FISHER So like my face is moving now?

JOHN *(as if in a slight reverie)* Mmm. Melting. Well yes.

DR FISHER So, Mr Moriatis...

JOHN *(zombie voice)* Moraitis.

DR FISHER ... I take it that you consider the effects of your drug-taking may impact on your duties as a soldier in Vietnam.

JOHN   I want to serve my country just like the next guy — *(leaning heavily into the doctor, in a slight zombie voice)* I thought I might be dangerous.

DR FISHER *(pulling away from him)* If you'd just care to step back into the waiting room, Mr em. Someone will be with you shortly.

John goes back to the waiting room. A woman receptionist hands him a piece of paper. He acts neutral. Then he looks at the audience and gives a triumphant grin and a thumbs-up. The other people in the waiting room turn their chairs to form the two aisles of a plane as a plane noise comes up.

36. FLIGHT. 1978

Jasmina, the company.

Lights up on Jasmina amongst rows of passengers on a plane, some asleep with masks over their eyes, some reading, some covered in blankets under the following announcement.

Captain's announcement in Japanese followed by English.

CAPTAIN 機長からご連絡いたします。当機は当初の遅れを取り戻し、成田空港への到着はスケジュール通り、日本時間午後１時20分を予定しております。ごゆっくり空の旅をお楽しみください。

This is your captain speaking. Just a quick announcement to say we've managed to pick up some speed, so our landing time at Narita Tokyo airport is still as scheduled... *(fade out)*

A light glows around Jasmina highlighting her, but subtly.

JASMINA *(to audience)* I'm going out to visit my father in Tokyo. We lead very different lives, but we both love working abroad. I've worked in Africa, Australia and the Caribbean as an actor, my first love, and as a scuba diving instructor, my other enduring passion. Scuba diving is like flying. There are mountains and valleys in the sea like on land and you can leap off a cliff underwater – pshhhh – and fly down the face of it, adjusting your buoyancy with your body and your breath. Or you can plunge, head down, pwwwwh... It's an incredible sensation to fly as it were, under water.

As Jasmina speaks the light changes and opens out, and the screen is filled with water, as the actors rise from their seats and metamorphose into fish. As the fish float past her, Jasmina reaches out to them, smiling.

JASMINA I used to touch, tickle and feed every sea creature I could, even sting rays; some were shy... some curious... some alarmed... none aggressive. *(to passing fish)* Oh you're a beauty! ... And look at you with your shimmery tail! Once, I rode on the largest fish in the sea – a whale shark – and in the Indian Ocean I rode on the back of a giant manta ray. (*Gently the fish evolve into an enormous manta ray as the light changes colour to evoke the light of the Indian Ocean.*)

(her voice now has a slight echo) Hovering above her I rest my hands lightly on her shoulders, her wing tips flick upwards, nervously, I stroke her gently, she's settling, we swim through a cloud of food as she shovels algae and plankton into her enormous mouth. She knows I'm there, she lets me ride on her, takes me. With her eight foot wing span, she swoops, banks slightly to the left, adjusts and we're diving...

CAPTAIN Ladies and gentlemen, we will shortly be starting our descent, please make sure your seat backs and tray tables are in their full upright position.

Under:

The giant manta ray actors rapidly collect up Jasmina's clothes and jewellery, and with their backs towards her create the tiny space of an aeroplane toilet. Now in great contrast to the previous section in the Indian Ocean we see Jasmina in a sharp square of light, changing and putting on make- up.

JASMINA Time to start dressing up as the Iranian ambassador's daughter. *(the image of her father with the Shah and the Queen comes up)* Oh, how I wish I spoke Farsi! – My mother's English, very English – brought up on the Sandringham estate, presented at court as a debutante – who married a Persian during the war. And I was brought up in London and New York. So... *(putting on her lipstick)* ... I'm a bit of a hybrid, never quite sure which half is the real me. *(gazing at self in mirror, then putting on a smart jacket and doing her hair in a chignon, and finally putting on a pearl necklace or ear rings)* Dad gave me these pearls. They don't exactly fit my life-style, but hey! There, that should do it.

As Jasmina makes her way to her seat, heads turn at her transformed appearance. As she sits down, a spotlight picks her out and the other passengers become less evident.

JASMINA Am I the daughter he wanted me to be, actor, explorer, scuba diving instructor? I know he's waiting to show me off in Japan, *(indicating her changed appearance)* hence all this. Pathetic isn't it, I'm 32 years old and still trying to please my father. Oh what the hell, I don't see him that often.

She stands up, and letting down her hair and removing her ear-rings transforms into the Jasmina of today, as music plays and the light closes around her.

JASMINA I'm glad I pleased him since Japan turned out to be his last posting. Soon after, the Iranian revolution broke out, the Shah *(image of the Shah comes up on the screen and remains till the end of the scene)* was deposed and my father came to England to retire. Three months later he died. Sadly I was advised that I, as his daughter, might now be a target, so we had this pitiful, private funeral for a man who had had an amazing life. As his coffin was lowered into the ground, a Pakistani paying his respects at another Muslim grave, saw us three non-Muslims, came over as a complete stranger, and said some prayers over my father's grave. And I'm sure this is not uncommon that our parents have extraordinary lives one way or another *(pauses as if lost in her own thoughts)* ... and then how small, how tiny it is when it's all over.

The image of the Shah is replaced by that of Ceauşescu for the next scene.

37. THE BIRTHDAY SPEECH.
Romania 1989

Imola, Theatre Director, the company.

On screen an image of a smaller image Ceauşescu as a framed picture.

The office of a theatre in Transylvania, Romania.

DIRECTOR *(at his desk, reading and editing his speech to himself)* 'To our much beloved...', much esteemed? *(writes in his correction)* 'To our much beloved, and greatly esteemed leader of the party and of our great country, who has worked for six decades...' No, no, 'Who has worked tirelessly for six decades to give this country prosperity and freedom, our dear comrade

Nicolae Ceauşescu, eminent revolutionary patriot, who is always deep in our hearts and in our thoughts, it is my great honour on this important occasion to wish you a very happy birthday!' *(a smug grunt)* Hmmmh.

He puts the speech down, looking pleased with himself. Imola arrives.

DIRECTOR Ah, Imola, Imola.

IMOLA Good morning Comrade Director.

DIRECTOR How nice to see you. Thank you so much for coming. *(indicates she should sit)* How are you?

IMOLA I'm fine thank you.

DIRECTOR Good, good, do sit down.

IMOLA Sorry I don't have too much time, my rehearsal starts in ten minutes.

DIRECTOR That's all right, this won't take long. Imola, you know how much we value your work in this theatre.

IMOLA Thank you.

DIRECTOR And so we have something very special in mind for you, a leading role, a monologue to be delivered on television in front of millions.

IMOLA It's a new role? What role is it?

DIRECTOR Ah, that's the unique thing about it. You'll be playing yourself.

IMOLA I don't understand.

DIRECTOR It's just one speech, which I have composed myself I might say, to be delivered by you, and you alone to our esteemed party leader and president Nicolae Ceauşescu on the occasion of his birthday.

(*No response. He hands her the speech.*) You will be representing not just our theatre but the whole theatrical profession in Romania.

IMOLA   It is a big honour for me.

DIRECTOR Indeed it is.

IMOLA   I think my Romanian is not good enough, it's not my first language.

DIRECTOR Your Romanian? What nonsense my dear. What about all those films you've done.

IMOLA   It's one thing to play a film role and quite another to give a speech on such a big occasion. My accent...

DIRECTOR Oh but your accent is charming and it also shows that you represent the Hungarian community in Romania and how much they love our esteemed leader.

Pause, then:

IMOLA   I'm really sorry but I don't feel mature enough for this honour, I'm not ready for it.

DIRECTOR But you are being too modest, my dear, you're our leading actress.

IMOLA   There are wonderful Romanian actors who could do it much better.

DIRECTOR But we are asking you. We are doing you this great honour.

Imola slowly packs away her glasses, then:

IMOLA   You know what – I'm not doing it.

DIRECTOR Why?

IMOLA   I don't want to.

DIRECTOR You don't want to!

IMOLA NO!

DIRECTOR What do you mean you don't want to! Who do you think you are to refuse this?

IMOLA *(silent)*

DIRECTOR You have no right to refuse this

IMOLA I have every right.

DIRECTOR If you refuse you are finished, and not just in this theatre.

IMOLA I'm going home.

DIRECTOR If you go home you will not return. You realise what you're doing to yourself? You realise what the implications are for your work here in this theatre?

IMOLA But my work is good. I've worked hard here for years.

DIRECTOR And now we are asking you to represent us which will bring huge kudos to our theatre.

IMOLA *(silent)*

DIRECTOR And if you don't do this I will break you.

IMOLA *(pause then, stands up)* I'm going home.

DIRECTOR *(shouts)* How dare you! You are finished.

Imola exits.

DIRECTOR *(shouts after her)* And not just in this theatre!

The actors crowd round Imola, as though to protect her, her proud demeanour now one of shock and fear. They shoot out one-liners:

ACTOR   You need a letter.

ACTOR   From a psychiatrist.

ACTOR   Saying you're mentally ill.

ACTOR   That's what you need now.

ACTOR   If you want to avoid a car accident.

ACTOR   If you don't want to end up hanging from a tree in the forest

ACTOR   Like that actor with the big mouth, you know, your friend whatshisname

ACTOR   Or?

ACTOR   Yes?

ACTOR   Ask your father to give you his car!

ACTOR   Yes!

ACTOR   Then drive across the border at night

ACTOR   I can't.

ACTOR   Of course she can't. How is she going to get her passport back from the police?

ACTOR   The letter then.

ACTOR   But no doctor will agree.

ACTOR   They're all too scared.

ACTOR   So she lies awake at night.

ACTOR   Waiting for something or nothing to happen.

ACTOR   And not long after, something does happen

Whisper passes round, a mixture of questions and statements:

ACTORS   Ceauşescu/Shot/Dead/Firing squad

ACTOR   The revolution happens.

IMOLA   And my mother is rushed to hospital

DOCTOR   Just a small heart attack

ACTOR   From excitement

DOCTOR   She'll be fine.

IMOLA   And joy.

Music to indicate end of section.

PART 5

"Ripeness is all" – mostly the 21st Century

38. ENDGAME. Wiener Library, London 2006

Narrator, Ruth.

NARRATOR 65 years after Ruth last saw her parents, she wanted to find out what happened to them. She knew they had been killed but she didn't know where or when. She visits the Wiener Library in London where they have a lot of material on the Holocaust. She meets two young German women who are working there, they are not Jewish, and they want to help her. They insist she sits down, relaxes and has some coffee.

RUTH An hour later they come out with two pieces of paper, one about my mother, one about my father, the Germans were good at documenting everything. My parents died in Treblinka, six months apart – they did not even have the comfort of dying together. My father was 34, my mother 32. I feel numb. I feel I am turning to stone, then I feel four hands reaching out to me, they are cradling me in their arms like I was a child again, two lovely young German women, so maybe, just maybe... there is some hope?

39. ENDGAME. Singapore 1993

Narrator, Annie, possibly plus the company as patients in a public ward in a Singapore hospital.

NARRATOR Annie's father lived to the fine age of ninety- two.

ANNIE After the Partition, of India from Pakistan, my father retired from the Army and re-settled in Singapore, with a new job as Chief of Civil Defence. There he married my step-mother, a hospital nurse originally from mainland China, who had survived harrowing times under the Japanese occupation. She was fiercely proud and possessive of "The Colonel", who she cared for and protected so jealously that my sister and I seldom saw him alone in all our years of summer visiting. When I flew out for what I knew would be the last time, I found him on a huge public ward with beds for perhaps a hundred patients, set out in rows under noisily whirring *punkas*.

The hubbub of a public ward with visitors bringing food.

My father lay with his eyes closed, under a thin sheet. Through it I could see how much he'd shrunk, this exceptional sportsman – he was set to represent the army in the pentathlon at the Olympic games in 1939 but it was cancelled because of the war – reduced now to bone and very little flesh. A carcass. I touched his face and he opened his eyes – they'd been so blue, now clouded and pale – and I knew he knew it was me, and that in this crowded place we were on our own together.

Conversation wasn't going to happen, so I read to him – rather madly in those alien surroundings – some of the nonsense rhymes he'd learned and loved to quote:

"The chief defect of Henry King/Was chewing little bits of string

At length he swallowed some which tied/itself in ugly knots inside".

And I sang to him, in my terrible tuneless voice – a German song he taught me when I was little, accompanying me on the penny-whistle that always travelled with him, even to the Khyber Pass. And hummed some of the Viennese waltzes he adored.

The next morning he died. I'm sure he'd waited for me. I think it was probably my awful singing that finished him off.

40. LEAR IN VIETNAM. Ho Chi Minh City 2012

John, Vietnamese schoolchildren and teacher, Vietnamese monk.

JOHN *(addressing the audience)* I finally got to Vietnam 40 years late, playing Lear to packed houses in Ho Chi Minh City. Kids would mob us after performances, asking for autographs, and they'd share a pen.

We see them handing round the solitary pen.

TEENAGER 1 Mr Lear sir.

TEENAGER 2 *(handing him a paper)* Please, your name?

TEENAGER 3 Me, me.

TEENAGER 4 Me Mr King.

TEACHER *(waving them away)* That's enough! Stop it! Stop it now.

The actors dash off to take their seats at the side of the stage.

JOHN *(walking through the outside area of the war museum)* Outside their War Museum – the Museum of War Remnants they call it – there's this whole collection of stuff the Americans left behind, tanks, F16s, helicopters, you name it, and then inside, there are black and white photographs of that period, the anti-Vietnam war demonstrations all over the world, including the US, and these photographs of young soldiers, you know, walking through the Mekong Delta, with water up to here, 19, 20 years old, that could have been me.

And there's this one picture of a young guy, maybe twenty years old holding up by the hair of its head the remnants of a body, just the torso, holding it up for the camera, while smoking a cigarette. And that's what they did to those kids, these were kids from New York City or Tulsa in Oklahoma and they made them into these killers. (*The photo comes up on screen.*) And I have to leave and get some air. It was so overwhelmingly emotional, it still is, to see what we did to those people, to see what that war did to my generation.

John walks away from the image abruptly, overcome. An elderly Vietnamese man is outside. He's wearing the saffron robe of a Buddhist monk. He observes John breathing deeply trying to recover.

MAN   You G.I.?

JOHN   Me? No. NO! But... people I knew. Young men. (*Beat.*) And you? What about you?

MAN *(mimes machine gunning)*

JOHN   Vietcong?

MAN *(nods)* Young men. *(gestures with his fingers 'crazy')* We like fight for our country. We like communism. Old men *(indicates John and himself)* more wise. *(pointing to his monk's robes)* Now I fight communist government. But not with gun.

Beat.

JOHN *(looking into the distance)* I never realized what a beautiful country, you have. We only saw war footage. I went to the Mekong Delta at the weekend. It's beautiful.

The man nods.

JOHN   You live in a monastery?

MAN   Of course.

JOHN   You still see your family though?

MAN   No. You live with your children?

JOHN   I don't have any children.

MAN   So who look after you now you are old? Wife?

JOHN   I'm not married. It's just me and my boat, the one I live on.

MAN *(smiling)* So you must do like me. *(indicates his robes)*

JOHN   I don't think I'm ready for that just yet. *(Beat.)* So you never married either?

MAN   Oh yes, I have three children, have wife, they all die. I was too busy. *(mimes machine-gunning)* So I hate war. And I come to this place, every day, this museum to meet people. Like you.

JOHN   Well I'm pleased I came here. I felt I had to. (*Beat.*) I guess I'll go back in now, see the rest. Good to meet you.

MAN (*makes a gesture of prayer*)

41. All RIGHT, DEAR? The Royal Free Hospital, London 2014

Ruth, Nurse, Dr Hunter.

A hospital corridor. Ruth is sitting on a chair, waiting. A nurse passes by.

NURSE (*sugary sweet*) Are you all right dear?

RUTH   Yes, thank you.

NURSE   Bless. The doctor won't be long now.

RUTH   Thank you.

Enter doctor.

DR HUNTER Mrs Posner, would you like to come with me.

RUTH   Are you the consultant?

DR HUNTER No, I'm afraid she's not available.

RUTH   Oh.

They enter consulting room and sit down.

DR HUNTER Right, so Mrs Posner, I understand you've been having breathing problems.

RUTH   Well yes I've been through all that with the nurse, and with the young lady who saw me just now. She also took my history.

He looks at his papers.

DR HUNTER Yes, yes of course she did. But if you wouldn't mind my asking you a few more questions?

RUTH   No, not at all. Sorry, you are?

DR HUNTER Dr Hunter. I'm the registrar. Right, so I have your date of birth here.

RUTH   Yes?

DR HUNTER So, my first question is... what day of the week is it?

RUTH   Pardon?

DR HUNTER I have to ask you this. Just routine.

RUTH   Well it's Wednesday.

DR HUNTER *(exaggerated)* Excellent! *(ticks a box)* And now, can you tell me the name of the Prime Minister?

RUTH   Sorry, I don't understand.

DR HUNTER The Prime Minister.

RUTH   No, no, I understand the word Prime Minister.

DR HUNTER *(ticks a box)* I'm intrigued by your accent Mrs Posner.

RUTH   I was born in Poland.

DR HUNTER Ah! But you speak English.

RUTH   After 64 years here, I should hope so. But please just don't ask me the name of the Polish prime minister.

DR HUNTER Ha ha. Well that's not on my list actually.

RUTH   Oh you have a list?

DR HUNTER Just a routine list, Mrs Posner, nothing personal.

RUTH My breathing is very personal to me actually, doctor, which is the reason I'm here.

DR HUNTER Of course, of course... And the prime minister's name, sorry to have to ask you?

RUTH Bloody Cameron! David Cameron.

DR HUNTER *(ticking a box)* Great! Right now I'd like to examine you if I may. *(over-solicitous)* I wonder if you could just hop up on this bed for me, it may be a bit high, do you need any help?

RUTH *(raising her leg high in the air)* I was trained as a dancer – and I've still got all my marbles!

DR HUNTER Wow!

Lighting change as Dr Hunter and Nurse return to their seats amongst the audience, whilst Ruth keeps her leg up.

RUTH How can I do this? *(lowers her leg)* And still feel joy? Exhilaration? Because I remember...

Segue into Epilogue

EPILOGUE

*On screen comes the title: Who Do We Think We Are?
Bare stage apart from Ruth on her chair. One by one the
actors come on stage with their first lines.*

JOHN *(entering, soft)* We remember...

RUTH *(strong)* ... my parents' love.

JASMINA *(soft)* My father's voice, warm, strong.

JOHN My father's voice – which I never heard.

ANDREW My father's voice, cut off in its prime – his rich brown actor's voice

NORMA My mother's voice. Flowing into me now.

TREVOR My father's voice, angry, his father's before him, flowing out of me now.

PAUL My father's voice – different inside me now.

ANDREW My voice. Released into me now. My voice.

TOGO *(Beat.)* We've remembered

ANNIE Tried to remember

JOHN The gulls on the rocky shore – the suitcase precariously lowered into the rowboat

JASMINA The mountains towering beneath the sea

NORMA Our Liverpool garden – lush in the afternoon sun

ANNIE The elephant at my party

IMOLA The wolf in the forest... *(The actors look at her surprised.)* I told you! Remember? *(Beat.)*

PAUL We've remembered

TOGO We think we've remembered

TREVOR   The body in the trench, in the bed, on the chair, the body furled...

TOGO *(as he bows)* Greeting my father every evening on the doorstep

TREVOR   ... for me to unfurl.

TOGO *(Greeting in Japanese, then unfurling from his bowing position. A beat.)*

JASMINA We've remembered journeys.

ANDREW Journeys of light and sun.

JOHN   Journeys across oceans, journeys to a better place,

PAUL   Journeys across continents,

RUTH   Journeys to dark places, journeys of escape.

NORMA   We've remembered

IMOLA   Love and war

RUTH   And hate – and love

JOHN   Love!

ANNIE   Dreams.

TREVOR   My dream of my father, coming towards me out of the dark, *(a spotlight makes its way towards Trevor in lieu of his father, Trevor's eyes following it till it comes right up to him)* the size of a small child, with the face of an old, old man, holding out to me a flower, and smiling a smile I never saw in his lifetime, so open, so full of warmth. *(looks down as though this diminutive figure of his father is next to him, mimes taking the flower)* Thank you. *(to fellow actors)* Thank you. *(to audience)* Thank you.

Lights down.

The End.

Aurora Metro Books

more great contemporary plays

THE ARAB-ISRAELI COOKBOOK PLAY by Robin Soans
ISBN 978-0-9542330-9-9   £7.99

WOMEN OF ASIA by Asa Palomera
ISBN 978-1-906582-94-4   £7.99

THE TROUBLE WITH ASIAN MEN by S.Bhuchar, K.Landon-Smith,
L.Wallinger ISBN 978-1-906582-41-8   £8.99

FROM THE MOUTHS OF MOTHERS by Amanda Stuart Fisher
ISBN 978-1-906582-99-9   £8.99

FROM DOCKS TO DESKTOPS by Simon Startin
ISBN 978-1-906582-54   £8.99

UNDER THEIR INFLUENCE by Wayne Buchanan
ISBN 978-0-9536757-5-3   £6.99

PROJECT XXX by Kim Wiltshire and Paul Hines
ISBN 978-1-906582-55   £8.99

THE DUTIFUL DAUGHTER by Charles Way in English and Mandarin
ISBN 978-0-9546912-6-4   £7.99

NEW SOUTH AFRICAN PLAYS ed. Charles J. Fourie
ISBN 978-0-9542330-1-3   £11.99

DURBAN DIALOGUES, INDIAN VOICE by Ashwin Singh
ISBN 978-1-906582-42-5   £15.99

BLACK AND ASIAN PLAYS Anthology introduced by Afia Nkrumah
ISBN 978-0-9536757-4-6   £12.99

BALKAN PLOTS: New Plays from Central and Eastern Europe
ed. Cheryl Robson ISBN 978-0-9536757-3-9   £9.95

EASTERN PROMISE: plays from central and eastern europe
eds. Sian Evans and Cheryl Robson ISBN 978-0-9515877-9-9   £12.99

www.aurorametro.com